THE NUCLEAR DEBATE

A Lehrman Institute Book

THE NUCLEAR DEBATE
Deterrence and the Lapse of Faith

ROBERT W. TUCKER

HM HOLMES & MEIER
New York · London

First published in the United States of America
1985 by
Holmes & Meier Publishers, Inc.
30 Irving Place
New York, N.Y. 10003

Great Britain:
Holmes & Meier Limited
Hillview House
One Hallswelle Parade
London NW11 ODL, England

Book design by Ellen Foos

Library of Congress Cataloging-in-Publication Data

Tucker, Robert W.
  The nuclear debate.

  (A Lehrman Institute book)
  1. Deterrence (Strategy)—Addresses, essays, lectures.   2. United States—Military policy—Addresses,
essays, lectures.   3. Nuclear warfare—Addresses,
essays, lectures.   I. Title.   II. Series.
U162.6.T83   1985   355'.0217   85-14007
ISBN 0-8419-1038-3
ISBN 0-8419-1039-1 (pbk.)

Manufactured in the United States of America

Contents

Lehrman Institute Books

THE LEHRMAN INSTITUTE was founded in 1972 as a private, nonprofit, operating foundation devoted to the analysis of public policy in its broadest aspects, with particular emphasis on the historical roots of contemporary policy questions. The Institute encourages interdisciplinary study—so as to foster a greater awareness of the interpretation of history, politics, and economics—and also contributes to nonpartisan debate on contemporary policy issues. To these ends, the Institute sponsors annually a program of seminars organized around the works-in-progress of a small number of Fellows and also conducts other series of study groups focusing on major problems in foreign affairs and economic policy. These seminars bring together scholars, businessmen, journalists, and public servants.

In 1976, the Institute began publishing books under its aegis that include specially commissioned essays and other monographs originally presented as working papers in Institute seminars and that, in the judgment of the Trustees of the Institute, are worthy of presentation to a wider public.

The Lehrman Institute does not take any position with regard to any issue: all statements of fact and expression of opinion in these publications are the sole responsibility of the individual authors.

Preface

SINCE THE EARLY 1980s we have had a continuing debate over nuclear weapons and their proper role in American strategy. This series of essays examines features of a debate that shows no promise of subsiding. The major theme of this volume is that the debate reveals a lapse of faith in the system of deterrence we have lived with for a generation. This lapse cannot be attributed primarily to the Reagan administration; its causes must be found elsewhere. Even so, it is now apparent that the administration itself has a declining faith in deterrence. A growing skepticism over deterrence is apparent in President Reagan's ardent support for the Strategic Defense Initiative.

Whether the present nuclear debate will end with the restoration of former faith in deterrence seems altogether doubtful. Certainly, it seems doubtful there will ever be quite the degree of confidence in the present system of deterrence. But what may, if anything, take the place of a lapsed faith is impossible to say at this time.

Two of the essays in this volume were presented at seminars at the Lehrman Institute as part of the Institute's ongoing studies program on national security issues. Parts of two of the essays earlier appeared in *Foreign Affairs* ("The Nuclear Debate," Fall 1984) and in *Ethics* ("Morality and Deterrence," April 1985) and are excerpted by permission of the publishers.

My colleagues at the Lehrman Institute, Michael Mandelbaum, Nicholas X. Rizopoulos, and Linda Wrigley helped me greatly at each stage of writing these essays. It is a pleasure to thank them here.

THE NUCLEAR DEBATE

DETERRENCE
Change and Continuity

In the almost four decades since the appearance of nuclear weapons, concern over the dangers these weapons raise has varied markedly. A preoccupation with nuclear weapons has characterized only a very few, and even among these few anxiety over the prospects of nuclear war has not been a constant. Beyond the nuclear strategists and a small entourage, the nuclear question has not evoked a steady level of attention, let alone of anxiety. On the contrary, the attention of foreign policy elites, and even more the general public, has swung from one extreme to the other and within a brief period of time.

Thus at the outset of the Kennedy administration, a preoccupation with the prospect of nuclear war characterized a portion of the foreign policy elites, but hardly the public at large. That preoccupation, in part the product of high and sustained international tension and in part the response to administration calls for measures of civil defense, quickly dissipated in the wake of the Cuban missile crisis. Within the period of scarcely a year it had virtually disappeared. Yet there had been no significant change in the strategic relationship between the United States and the Soviet Union. Nor had the arms competition between the two powers been significantly altered. Cer-

3

tainly the 1963 partial test ban did not alter this competition, by making it either less intense or less dangerous than it had earlier been. But the test ban did signal that the political relationship between the two states had changed modestly for the better and might register still further improvement. A substantial and even dramatic change in outlook toward the prospects of nuclear war went hand in hand with a changing political relationship.

A generation later, the same process, only now working in the opposite direction, marked the outset of the Reagan administration. On this occasion, an anti-nuclear weapons movement developed that was unprecedented in the breadth of support it appeared to enjoy. In this respect, there is no real comparison between the anti-nuclear movement of a generation ago and that of today. Whereas the movement of yesterday represented little more than the stirring of a few, the movement of the 1980s assumed mass proportions. The later movement was also distinguished by the greater activity it evoked. In the 1980s, people did more to express their anxiety over nuclear weapons. Not only did they sign petitions and give money, many of them took (however decorously) to the streets. They did so, in the main, over the proposal to freeze the deployment, testing, and manufacture of all nuclear weapons by both superpowers. Moreover, once the nuclear issue had suddenly resurfaced—whether in the form of the freeze or in a more general manner—it became politicized in a way that it never really did in the 1950s and early 1960s.

The most impressive evidence, though, for the unprecedented character of the 1980s anti-nuclear weapons movement is the effect it had on the administration that many critics hold responsible for having given birth to it. Although initially both insensitive and resistant to public anxiety on the nuclear issue, after scarcely a year in office the Reagan administration began to respond to public concern. Since early 1982, the record shows that it has consistently felt the need to adjust its policies, not just its rhetoric, to placate this concern. In an earlier period, by contrast, for all the international outcry about the atmospheric testing of nuclear weapons, President Eisenhower never stopped testing and President Kennedy, having once stopped testing, resumed doing so when the Soviet government broke the moratorium. Nor did the 1963 treaty forbidding atmospheric testing result from a groundswell of public opposition to testing. Instead, the treaty came as a result of the Cuban missile crisis. The personal project of Kennedy and Krushchev, the American promoters worried that they would fail to secure its ratification and, accordingly, launched an elaborate campaign to rally support for it.

The differences between the two anti-nuclear weapons movements we have experienced to date point to the changes that have occurred over a generation in the public's attitude toward nuclear arms (and, more generally, toward the nation's security).[1] Of immediate relevance here, however, is not so much the nature and significance of these changes as the abruptness with which they became manifest. The appearance of the later movement was almost as sudden as the disappearance of the earlier one. As late as the winter of 1979–80 there was little to indicate that nuclear weapons would become the critical issue of public life and discourse they did become by the summer of 1981.

The sudden rise in this decade of the anti-nuclear weapons movement and the attendant debate over nuclear strategy must be attributed in the first place to a renewed fear of war with the Soviet Union. The same fear gave rise, for the most part, to the movement of a generation ago. Then, as later, it was almost universally assumed that armed conflict between the superpowers, however it might begin, would end with the use of nuclear weapons. The peace movement of the 1980s is often characterized by its champions as one directed against nuclear war. The characterization is true enough as far as it goes. But it does not go far enough. Every antiwar movement has been directed against war, just as every antiwar movement has also been a response to the prospect of a particular war. Without this prospect, the ranks of peace movements would have to be filled entirely by those who are pacifists in principle, and they have never been numerous enough to be politically significant. It may be argued that with respect to the prospect of nuclear war, this is

---

1. Cf. Daniel Yankelovich and John Doble, "The Public Mood: Nuclear Weapons and the U.S.S.R.," *Foreign Affairs* (Fall 1984), pp. 33–46.

no longer the case, and that so-called nuclear pacifism commands a following never enjoyed by pre-nuclear pacifism. It is by no means clear whether this view is well taken. Even if it is, the point remains that the peace movement of the 1980s is a response to the prospect of a particular war.

Whatever else it may portend, then, the recent anti-nuclear movement evidently reflected a reawakened fear of war with the Soviet Union. By the same token, it also reflected a decline in the faith by which we have come to live in the nuclear age. For we are nearly all believers in deterrence, and this despite the different ways in which this faith may be expressed. We are nearly all believers if only for the reason that once we seriously admit nuclear war as a distinct historical possibility, we conjure up not only a very dark landscape but one in which our accepted categories of political and moral thought no longer seem relevant. In the still alien world of nuclear weapons, it is only a faith in deterrence that preserves continuity with a familiar past.[2]

The idea of deterrence—that is, of prevention by threat of retaliation—is of course as old as the history of human conflict. But the functions that strategies of nuclear deterrence are expected to serve and the expectations these strategies have raised are as novel as the weapons on which deterrence today rests. If nuclear deterrence is indeed something new under the sun, it is so not only because of the weapons but because of the expectations it has evoked. These expectations constitute the core of faith and their intensity has invested nuclear deterrence with a reliability that is tantamount, for all practical purposes, to certainty. In turn, faith in the effectiveness of deterrence is largely a function of the consequences generally expected to follow from the use of nuclear weapons. By a psychological mechanism as simple as it is pervasive, it is assumed that if the results of an act are inconceivable, the act itself must be inconceivable. The death

---

2. At the outset of the missile age, the man who was later to become a hero to the deterrence faithful remarked: "The strategy of deterrence ought always to envisage the possibility of deterrence failing." Bernard Brodie, *Strategy in the Missile Age* (Princeton: Princeton University Press, 1959), p. 292. Experience has shown the very great difficulty of reconciling this injunction with a faith in deterrence.

of a nation is an event difficult to conceive, and the extinction of humanity far more so.

Nor is this all. It is faith in the effectiveness of deterrence that has enabled us to entertain what otherwise would prove to be irreconcilable convictions. A continued readiness to threaten the use—even the first use—of nuclear weapons to preserve interests deemed vital, but at the same time a conviction that nuclear war would in all likelihood destroy the ends for which it is waged; a belief if not in the moral rectitude then at least in the moral neutrality of a deterrent strategy, but also a disbelief that the use of nuclear weapons could ever be morally justified; these and other convictions can be reconciled if only the expectations placed in a deterrent strategy are strong enough. With enough faith in deterrence there is no need to torture oneself over the justification for ever employing nuclear weapons; the issues arising from the use of these weapons deal with a contingency that has been virtually excluded from our vision of the future.

The faith commonly placed in deterrence has never gone unquestioned. The history of strategic thought in the nuclear age is, after all, a history of the persisting controversy between the deterrence faithful and the deterrence skeptics, between those who believe that deterrence follows from the existence of nuclear weapons and those who believe a credible theory of use must be developed if deterrence is to be assured. The nature of that controversy is often misrepresented, not least of all by the participants themselves. It cannot properly be characterized simply as one "between those who wish to give nuclear weapons a war-deterring and those who want to give them a war-fighting role."[3] Those accused of wishing to give nuclear weapons a war-fighting role have not abandoned deterrence. At least, they have never admitted to doing so. Instead, they insist that the effort to fashion a war-fighting role for nuclear weapons, however precarious and even abortive that effort may ultimately prove, is undertaken in the first instance in order to enhance their role as a deterrent. The deterrence skeptics do not

---

3. Theodore Draper, "Nuclear Temptations," *The New York Review of Books* (January 19, 1984), p. 43.

deny deterrence. They do deny a faith that is given, in the manner of all true believers, unconditional expression.

To the deterrence faithful, the position of the skeptics has always smacked of apostasy and perhaps never more so than today. To be sure, the faithful no less than the skeptics have regularly warned against the dangers of taking deterrence for granted. Still, there is a world of difference between what skeptics have understood taking deterrence for granted to mean and what true believers have understood it to mean. To the latter, deterrence is not only an inherent property of nuclear weapons, it is very nearly a self-sufficient property. "The strategy," one of them declares, "is determined by the weapon. The missiles have only to exist and deterrence is the law of their existence."[4] Deterrence is the law of their existence by virtue of their inordinate and uncontrollable destructiveness. Given this destructiveness, the failure of deterrence is not the beginning but the end of strategy. This being so, if deterrence fails the only rational course is to end the conflict as quickly as possible and without regard to calculations of relative advantage. McGeorge Bundy, in a recent elaboration of the concept of "existential deterrence," echoes the well-known dictum of Bernard Brodie in declaring that if deterrence ever breaks down, "the attention of both sides must be driven toward the literally vital need for *ending* the nuclear battle if possible, not winning it."[5]

The controversy over the necessary and sufficient conditions of deterrence is as intense today as it has ever been. This

---

4. Leon Wieseltier, *Nuclear War, Nuclear Peace* (New York: Holt, Rinehart & Winston, 1983), p. 38. This is, of course, the essential rationale for "existential deterrence." At the dawn of the nuclear age, Bernard Brodie provided the first formulation of existential deterrence in observing that "everything about the atomic bomb is overshadowed by the twin facts that it exists and that its destructive power is fantastically great." *The Absolute Weapon* (New York: Harcourt Brace, 1945), p. 52.

5. McGeorge Bundy, "The Bishops and the Bomb," *The New York Review of Books* (June 10, 1983), p. 4. In an essay written at the end of his life, Bernard Brodie declared that: "The main war goal upon the beginning of a strategic nuclear exchange would surely be to terminate it as quickly as possible and with the least amount of damage possible—on both sides." "The Development of Nuclear Strategy," *International Security* (Spring 1978), p. 79.

persisting debate does not in the end turn on technical considerations, though the disputants regularly foster that mistaken impression. Instead, what is ultimately at issue are varying judgements about the character and aspirations of the Soviet regime and, to a lesser extent, the American government. Whether asymmetries in strategic systems have political significance, whether some capacity for war-fighting is a necessary element of deterrence, are not issues that, at bottom, can be resolved by technical considerations but only by one's assessment of the two great nuclear adversaries. Among the priesthood of experts, the nuclear debate is not primarily a debate over nuclear weapons but a debate over politics. In this debate, both sides share a common faith; but how they interpret the conditions of faith depends on what they believe to be the truth about the Soviet-American conflict.

Thus, for all their differences, which are surely serious enough, the two sides to this familiar controversy not only believe in deterrence, they also believe broadly in the strategic status quo and are hostile to apocalyptic visions. By contrast, such visions are a hallmark of the anti-nuclear movement that arose in the early 1980s. The view that nuclear war has become ever more likely, and that if we continue along our present course we will transform a possibility into a probability, is given frequent expression. Time alone is found to lead to this result. Jonathan Schell has attributed the "collapse of deterrence" to nothing other than the buildup of nuclear stockpiles. "Possession inevitably implied use," he declares, "and use was irremediably senseless."[6] The crisis in deterrence stems, at bottom, from nothing more than the "continuing reliance on nuclear arms." George Kennan reaches a similar conclusion and attaches to it similar urgency. "The clock is ticking; the remaining ticks are numbered; the end of their number is already in sight."[7]

We may call this view that of "existential disaster." Nuclear weapons have only to exist in sufficient numbers and destruc-

---

6. Jonathan Schell, "Reflections: The Abolition," *The New Yorker* (January 2, 1984), pp. 64–5.

7. George Kennan, *The Nuclear Delusion* (New York: Pantheon Books, 1983), p. 231.

tiveness to render disaster likely. Time is the great nemesis. It is so if only because no social contrivance—of which deterrence is one—can go on indefinitely without a breakdown. This conviction was first articulated a generation earlier. In 1961, the novelist and scientist C. P. Snow wrote: "Within, at the most, ten years, some of these bombs are going off. . . . *That* is the certainty. On the one side, therefore, we have a finite risk. On the other side we have a certainty of disaster. Between a risk and a certainty, a sane man does not hesitate."[8] Snow's forecast was made in the same spirit and on behalf of the same purpose—far-reaching measures of arms control—that today move Jonathan Schell and George Kennan. But whereas Snow's message could only be directed profitably to a quite restricted audience, Schell and Kennan have a potential audience that is far larger. And while Snow's prophecy was one of limited catastrophe, Schell and Kennan entertain a vision of a nuclear exchange that would "put an end to our own species."[9]

What is at once apparent in considering the nuclear debate that arose in the 1980s is its continuity with the past. Although a generation had elapsed since the last major debate over nuclear weapons, the questions raised on this later occasion have been largely the same questions that were raised earlier. What are the requirements of deterrence? Can these requirements be met indefinitely and, even if they can, at what political and moral cost? Are they compatible in the long run with the political institutions and moral foundations of a liberal-democratic society? What happens if deterrence fails? Can nuclear weapons be employed to achieve any of the traditional objectives of war? If they can, why has a plausible scenario of a nuclear conflict not been devised? If they cannot, must not the breakdown of deterrence be attended by the determination to stop the ensuing

8. C. P. Snow, "The Moral Un-neutrality of Science," *Science* (January 27, 1961), p. 259.

9. Schell, "Reflections: The Abolition," p. 44.

conflict and to do so without regard to considerations of relative advantage? But quite apart from the intrinsic difficulty of crediting a strategy—deterrence—that has only this response to the contingency of its breakdown, does not the quick termination of the conflict depend on the parallel behavior if not the agreement, of both sides? If only one side moves to terminate the conflict, however, may it not be placed at a great and perhaps even fatal disadvantage?

It is not only the questions that have remained by and large the same. The answers, too, have remained the same and they seem no more satisfactory than they did on an earlier occasion. (The only apparently novel answer has been one that addresses itself not to resolving the dilemmas of deterrence but to transcending them through the promise of a defense against all nuclear weapons, whatever their means of conveyance.)

None of this should prove surprising. Our political and moral thought is predicated on the assumption of limits. Nuclear weapons challenge this assumption by virtue of their destructiveness and, of course, their rate of destruction. The view that the political and moral standards applied to judge prenuclear weapons must be equally applicable in judging nuclear weapons, that nuclear force simply represents a new quantitative dimension in the application of these perennial standards, is as true as it is irrelevant to the claim that nuclear conflict raises novel, and seemingly insoluble, issues. The novelty of these issues and the difficulty of dealing with them do not result from the absence of criteria affording a basis for political and moral judgement. They are instead, the result of the disparity between standards affording a basis for judgement and the consequences expected to attend the employment of nuclear weapons. Nor would the disparity even arise if these standards were not at some point vitally dependent upon, and made meaningful by, quantitative considerations. The political and moral novelty of the issues posed by nuclear war is as simple as it is profound. By introducing a new quantitative dimension into the conduct of war, by holding out the prospect of a war that might escape any meaningful limitation, nuclear weapons take the standards heretofore applied to force and threaten to make a hollow mockery of them.

Deterrence escapes these considerations only so long as the possibility of its breakdown is either denied or simply ignored. If the reliability of deterrence arrangements is believed to approach certainty, the only issues that can arise will concern deterrence and not nuclear war. In a world of perfect or near-perfect deterrence one may still question the long term effects on a society of relying on a deterrent strategy. Many have persistently done so since the 1950s, warning that these effects are bound to prove politically and morally corrosive. For a generation, their warnings went largely unheard. In the 1980s, they were given a new hearing, although such evidence as we have to date does not afford any greater support for this position than it did before. Quite the contrary, our experience indicates that so long as deterrent arrangements are looked upon with confidence they have little or no adverse effect on the societies supporting them, and this quite apart from the nature of the threat on which deterrence rests. At any rate, of themselves, these issues will not challenge the foundations of faith.

Even the champions of pure and simple deterrence, have seldom been so indiscreet as to endow deterrent strategies with certainty. No social contrivance can be invested with certainty. All are flawed. All may fail, including deterrence. But once this is acknowledged, the difficulties that a faith in deterrence had managed to exorcize reappear, and in acute form. If a deterrent strategy may fail, it is absurd to refuse to consider seriously the possible consequences of failure beyond saying that all effort must be directed to bringing the conflict to an end as quickly as possible and without regard to any other considerations. Equally, if a deterrent strategy may fail, it is absurd to insist upon using and justifying the threat of nuclear war as an instrument of policy but to deny that any meaningful or just purpose could be served by such a war.

These apparent absurdities have nevertheless formed part of the nuclear dialogue from the start. They continue to do so today. It is easy enough to call attention to them. But what is the alternative to them? One, we have long been told, is frankly to acknowledge nuclear war as a distinct historical possibility. Having done so, though, what is the character of this possibility? After endless speculation and debate we still cannot say with any assurance. The actual character of nuclear war remains as

obscure today as in the 1950s. It may well be, as Lawrence
Freedman concludes in his history of nuclear strategy that: "The
question of what happens if deterrence fails is vital for the intellectual cohesion and credibility of nuclear strategy." Yet Freedman also concludes: "It now seems unlikely that such an answer
can be found."[10]

Once nuclear war is frankly acknowledged as a distinct historical possibility, we are also compelled to ask yet again these
political-moral questions that force has always raised. The answers seem no more satisfactory today, however, than they
seemed a generation ago. Despite the technological changes that
have since occurred, and that have kindled hopes either of substantially moderating the nuclear dilemma or even of transcending it altogether, the basic dimensions of that dilemma
appear unchanged. Now as then, the essence of the nuclear
dilemma is one of limits.

What is new about the nuclear debate of the 1980s is not the
substance of the debate but the circumstances in which it
has taken place. The principal circumstance is, of course, the
changed nature of the strategic relationship between the United
States and the Soviet Union. A generation ago, this relationship
was still one that conferred a distinct advantage on the United
States. Today, it no longer does so. Instead, the claim has been
insistently made since the late 1970s that this former relationship has since been reversed and that it is the Soviet Union that
now enjoys an advantaged strategic position relative to its adversary. The Reagan administration came to office insistent on
the reality of this reversal and on the considerable dangers it
posed. Whatever the merit of this claim, and it has been bitterly
contested by a host of critics, there is no disagreement over the

10. Lawrence Freedman, *The Evolution of Nuclear Strategy* (New York: St.
Martin's Press, 1983), p. 395. Fred Kaplan, *The Wizards of Armageddon* (New York:
Simon and Schuster, 1983), p. 391, reaches the same conclusion: "The nuclear
strategists had come to impose order—but in the end chaos prevailed." See also
Michael Mandelbaum, *The Nuclear Question: The United States and Nuclear
Weapons, 1946–1976* (New York: Cambridge University Press, 1979), p. 127.

proposition that the United States no longer holds the strategic advantage it once did.

Along with this change has gone a change in public attitude toward nuclear weapons. To be sure, changes in attitude on such complex issues as this are nearly always attended by uncertainty and no little controversy. Even so, there seems little doubt but that a striking change in attitude has occurred and that, in consequence, the public now takes a far less acquiescent view toward nuclear weapons than it once did. Nuclear weapons are no longer seen to strengthen the nation's security. Instead, they are increasingly found to have weakened it. Along with this negative judgement has gone an equally negative judgement on the usability of nuclear weapons. The public neither approves their first use nor believes that if they are once used their use can be limited in a meaningful way. At the same time, an increasingly skeptical attitude toward nuclear weapons has been marked by a growing conviction that, whatever the future of arms control, nuclear weapons are here to stay. Their permanence is found tolerable on condition that we become less reliant on them.[11]

In varying degree, these public views are held by elites as well. The latter, too, have increasingly come to believe that nuclear weapons represent a net threat to our security. Although divided on the issue of whether we should continue to leave any real doubt that we would ever resort to the first use of nuclear weapons, widespread skepticism persists over the possibility of using these weapons in a limited manner. Finally, among elites the moral case against nuclear weapons has gained ever greater acceptance with the passage of time. Along with a growing inclination to deny moral legitimacy to any nuclear conflict we are likely to wage, has also gone a growing inclination to question the legitimacy of deterrent structures. This moral questioning of

---

11. Yankelovich and Doble, "The Public Mood," pp. 37–8. These findings are based on a National Agenda Survey that includes a substantial number of leading national surveys of public attitudes taken over a period of several years. Significantly, Yankelovich and Doble note that although the public now fully realizes the "present standoff between us and the Soviets . . . they have not yet thought through the strategic and policy implications of this awesome change in the rules" (p. 45).

both the use and the threat of nuclear weapons may well prove to be in the end the most significant development of all.

The anti-nuclear weapons movement and the attendant nuclear debate arose within this general setting. Although triggered in large measure by careless words of Reagan administration officials, the movement and controversy are the results of developments that can scarcely be laid at the doorstep of this administration. To argue that the emergence of the nuclear issue in the 1980s can be seen as the work of a misguided administration during its first years in office is to misunderstand the deeper significance of recent events and the portent they may well hold out. Although the activity of the anti-nuclear movement has clearly abated, the basic circumstances conditioning the explosive emergence of the nuclear issue have not diminished. If anything, they may be expected to grow stronger with the passage of time.

They may be expected to grow stronger if only because of the mounting debate today over the Reagan administration's Strategic Defense Initiative (SDI). Although the ultimate aim and promise of this initiative are to transcend the age of deterrence, the immediate effect is quite likely to erode further an already eroded faith. For the question must be asked: why undertake a very costly and—to the adversary—provocative, though ultimately uncertain, arms program unless one's faith in today's structures of deterrence is lacking? It is not enough to answer, as the President and his supporters have done, by pointing to the moral implications of these deterrent structures. A threat that would be evil to carry out may present serious problems for the moralist. But if the prospects of ever having to carry it out are negligible, it is only the moralist who is likely to be troubled. The emphasis on the moral perils of deterrent strategies can only suggest that the prospects of these strategies failing are not negligible. The defense initiative, and particularly its more ambitious goals, is difficult to understand save on the grounds that those promoting it have come to view deterrence with increasing skepticism.

DETERRENCE AND MORALITY
The Erosion of Legitimacy

W<small>E LIVE IN THE AGE</small> of deterrence. It is deterrence that constitutes the limiting condition of all our lives. And it is deterrence that forms the object of the faith by which we have come to live. At the same time, there have always been those unhappy with this faith. In recent years their numbers have increased. Their unhappiness is not to be equated simply with disbelief in the effectiveness of deterrence, though a number of them have experienced a decline in faith. It must also be attributed to the conviction that deterrence represents a fall from grace and that it constitutes a kind of moral purgatory, a state of near sin from which we should do our utmost to escape. Of late, this conviction has intensified and spread. So too has the belief that the legitimacy of deterrent structures can be no more than provisional, their justification even then depending upon the progress with which the great nuclear powers move toward escaping from the age of deterrence. Yet with the exception of those who believe that technology will deliver us from the nuclear predicament, the prospects for escaping the age of deterrence appear to be virtually nonexistent. Hence the growing unhappiness over what seems to be a near permanent state of things.

Deterrence not only persists as a common object of faith, it

17

is the contemporary embodiment of what an enlightened age was supposed to exorcize: reason of state. Indeed, deterrence forms what may be considered as the perfect—certainly, the extreme—expression of reason of state. It is the ultimate manifestation of the necessity that is ostensibly imposed on the statesman and that is justified in terms of the security and independence of the state and of those values the state protects. Deterrence lays bare the nature of reason of state as it has never before been laid bare. It illuminates with an almost burning intensity the paradoxes and contradictions of that doctrine. Finally, it points to the depressing truth that we are today as far away as ever from fashioning a satisfactory and viable alternative to this ancient plea.

What is the idea of the state's *ratio*? It is simply that there is at any particular moment in history, a certain course or pattern of action that is best calculated to preserve the state's independence and continuity. This course of action *is* the state's reason and to act in accordance with it is presumably a necessity that is imposed on the statesman. In the words of Friedrich Meinecke, reason of state "tells the statesman what he must do to preserve the health and strength of the state."[1] To follow it, he adds, is not a matter of choice but of "iron necessity."

The action required by reason of state may prove extreme. The distinctive problem raised by reason of state is how such conduct as may be required to safeguard the state's independence and continuity may be justified. For unless the appeal to necessity as such is considered sufficient to put an end to this matter, the problem of justification must be addressed. Of course, one way of addressing this problem is precisely by insisting that it is meaningless. Since the conduct in question belongs to the realm of necessity, it makes no more sense to pass

---

1. Douglas Scott, trans., *Machiavellism: The Doctrine of Raison d'Etat and Its History* (New Haven: Yale University Press, 1957), pp. 1–3.

moral judgement on it than it would to pass moral judgement on some catastrophe—an earthquake or flood—occurring in nature. These catastrophes may be seen as tragic, but they do not pose moral dilemmas for they are neither just nor unjust. So too, the actions taken to preserve the state may be seen as tragic, but they do not pose moral dilemmas for they are neither just nor unjust.

The theme of necessity in statecraft is at once very old yet very contemporary. There are many versions of it, the most recent and pervasive version being technology. The conviction that technology is a despot that increasingly presides over the destinies of men and nations has almost assumed the status today of a received truth. What continues to provoke sharp debate is only whether technology is a benevolent or a malevolent despot.

Although technology provides today the most persuasive version of necessity in statecraft, it does not exclude other and older versions. In a way, technology gives these older versions a new persuasiveness. If there is a necessity imposed by technology, it is because there is a necessity imposed by human nature and by the historical situation in which this nature must somehow act. Human nature and historical situation evidently set limits to what the statesman may do. But these limits do not establish the argument of necessity in a literal sense and the view that they do has seldom been consistently undertaken. Despite its attractions, the appeal to necessity is almost invariably applied in a selective manner and almost never with consistency. Clearly, at the root of this view is not only an explanation but a choice. The necessity imposed on the statesman turns out to be a "moral necessity" enjoining him to do that which is necessary to preserve the state's independence and survival. What appears as a necessity does so because a moral choice has already been made.

Yet it may be, and has regularly been, asked, how meaningful is this choice when the issue is one of independence and survival? Is there not a point, as John Stuart Mill noted with respect to the individual's claim to physical security, where freedom and necessity seem almost to converge, where "*ought* and *should* grow into *must,* and recognized indispensability becomes a moral necessity, analogous to physical, and often not inferior to it in binding force."[2] Moreover, given the distinctive and unchanging features of international society, Mill's observation evidently carries greater persuasion than it does in relation to the individual within civil society. What Hobbes considered the right of self-preservation that men once had in a state of nature, the argument of necessity considers the right of self-preservation that states have in the state of nature from which they have never emerged.[3]

The appeal to necessity is not incompatible with the acceptance of restraints on state action, so long as these restraints do not jeopardize the independence and survival of the political collective. But whether restraints can be observed and the nature of the restraint that can be observed will depend upon circumstances and not upon abstract considerations. To insist that certain restraints must always be observed if for no other reason than that they can always be observed without vital sacrifice, is to express an optimism that may or may not be justified. When it is not justified, a choice—if one may still call it that—must be made. It is but a further consequence of the state of nature that the manner in which this choice is exercized is left to the judgement of the interested parties.

There is no difficulty in cataloguing the many abuses to which the doctrine of reason of state has led. These abuses are not accidental; they are built into the very character of the doctrine.

---

2. John Stuart Mill, *Utilitarianism*, 15th ed. (London: J. M. Dent and Sons, 1907), p. 81.

3. Because, Hobbes wrote, in a state of nature "it is in vain for a man to have a right to the end, if the right to the necessary means be denied him, it follows that since every man hath a right to preserve himself, he must also be allowed a right to use all the means, and do all the actions, without which he cannot preserve himself." *The English Works of Thomas Hobbes,* vol. 4. *De Corpore Politico,* art. I, chap. I., sec. vii, p. 83.

This is so if only for the reason that the political collective forms a "self" the nature of which has always given rise to uncertainty and dispute. We may know where this self begins, we do not know—or, at any rate, can seldom agree—where it properly ends. The collective's physical self—its territory and population—has seldom been considered an adequate definition of the self. Instead, the collective's existence has regularly been considered to have dimensions other and greater than its merely physical attributes. A nation, it is said, may preserve its body yet perish through the loss of its soul or the abandonment of its purpose. This extension of the natural self is particularly apparent in the case of great nations. Indeed, it forms a part of their "natural history." And it goes a long way toward explaining why the necessities of great powers have nearly always been quite different from the necessities of small powers.

Even when the dimensions of the collective self are not extended beyond physical attributes, the potential for abusing an ostensibly narrow version of reason of state remains considerable. It does so in the main because the circumstances of international society prompt states to identify their security with their survival. If the state compels individuals to distinguish sharply between their security and their survival, it also enables them to do so. Between an immediate and less than immediate threat to the self stands the protective institutions of the state. In the absence of these protective institutions, quite different conclusions may be and have been drawn. Where security is not effectively collectivized, the distinction between security and survival remains tenuous. What seems to be an unnecessary and unreasonable projection of survival in civil society may appear necessary and reasonable in international society. While there is much to be said for this position, its acceptance must open the door to all kinds of abuses.

It does not follow that it is meaningless to speak of the self-preservation or survival of states. Although the analogy so often drawn between individual and collective has misled more than it has informed, states do face threats to their independence and survival. They do have to contend with an environment that may make difficult the drawing of a clear distinction between security and survival. The same environment may also make difficult the observance of restraints, if such observance is found to jeopardize the state's independence and continuity.

The doctrine of reason of state declares that when this is the case all other considerations should be subordinated to the safety of the state. Experience has shown that the governments of democratic states are as prepared to follow this doctrine as are the governments of non-democratic states. It is of course true that the distinctive justification of reason of state will differ in the two instances. A liberal-democratic society can scarcely find in the state the source of all value. But it may and does find in the state the indispensable condition of value. Our statesmen have uniformly urged that the purposes and objectives of American foreign policy may be properly understood only as a means to the end of protecting and promoting individual freedom and well-being. No end of foreign policy, then, can be self-justifying, an end in itself. Instead, all ends of foreign policy must be seen as means to the ends of society, which are in turn ultimately the ends of individuals. In theory, this is a critical difference, since in the one case the state is self-justifying whereas in the other case it has only a conditional justification. This conditional justification may break down and the state's "necessities" may be denied when it no longer effectively protects and promotes individual and cultural values but instead threatens to destroy those values that must sanction not only its actions but its very existence.

In practice, however, the above difference may have only a limited significance. How limited it will prove to be depends upon the importance attached to the state as a means to the protection and promotion of individual values. If the independence and survival of the state are also regarded as the indispensable means to the protection and promotion of individual values, how meaningful is it to insist that the state has no more than an instrumental value? If the state is not simply a condition but an indispensable condition of value, what is the practical significance of distinguishing between this institution as a source of value and as a condition of value? For all practical purposes, a condition of value which is nonetheless indispensable as a condition might just as well be regarded as a source of value.

Even a democratic version of reason of state, then, need admit of no limits to the measures that may be taken to preserve the political community's independence and continuity. Its necessity may reach out to take and to justify the same extreme measures as the necessity of non-democratic states. Are there, in either case, any limits to the measures that may be taken to preserve the state's independence and continuity? This is, of course, the crucial question reason of state has always raised. The answer has been regularly obscured. But when it has been candidly made, that answer has been that there are no limits. Thus it is not the abuse to which the argument of necessity so readily lends itself that is its profoundly disturbing feature but the refusal to acknowledge any restraints on the measures that may be taken on behalf of the state. The argument of necessity does not leave the critical issue of means unresolved. On the contrary, it is precisely in the manner by which this issue is in principle resolved that the distinctive character of "necessity of state" must be found.

Any serious critique of necessity must be directed to the critical issue of means. While not simply abandoning statecraft and its distinctive means, this critique must seek to impose limits on the alleged necessities of the state. It must seek to limit the distinctive means of statecraft, not to abandon these means. The issue of means may of course be resolved simply by abandoning the *ultima ratio* of statecraft. Pacifism has always formed one response to necessities of state and continues to do so today. But it does so by renouncing altogether the threat or use of force. Pacifism has often been defended as another kind, a different and higher kind, of policy. In fact, it is the abandonment of policy, for it is the abandonment of the means distinctive to statecraft. In refusing to threaten a potential aggressor with retributive measures, more generally, in refusing to confront an adversary with the prospect of returning like for like, pacifism disavows the principle of reciprocity so vital to the conduct of statecraft.

In contrast to pacifism, the ancient doctrine and tradition of the Roman Catholic Church does set itself the goal of imposing limits on the means permitted to the statesman and, in consequence, of prescribing what constitutes the just conduct of war. Without abandoning the distinctive means of statecraft, while acknowledging that the state does have its necessities and that they must be viewed as legitimate, this doctrine of *bellum justum* nevertheless insists that these necessities are circumscribed and that even when acting in defense of the state's independence and survival there are certain restraints that a government is never justified in exceeding.

In the U.S. Catholic bishops' pastoral letter on war and peace in the nuclear age we have a recent and impressive effort in a tradition that has been in Western thought perhaps the principal alternative to the plea of reason of state.[4] The bishops observe that the source of their doctrine is independent of and superior to the state and its necessities. At the same time, they both acknowledge and emphasize those necessities for the preservation of key values. Still, they are insistent that even for the preservation of these values certain measures may never be justified.

The reaction of the Reagan administration to the bishops' strictures ranged from one of unease to opposition. Indeed, in the relationship that developed between the bishops and the administration, we have an illustration of the conflict between reason of state and the attempts to limit the state's real or alleged necessities, though how pointed the conflict in fact was on this occasion is a matter deserving consideration. We will return to this recent example of an age-old conflict.

The Christian doctrine of *bellum justum* is addressed to both the justification for resorting to force and to the permitted

---

4. The Pastoral Letter of the U.S. Bishops on War and Peace, "The Challenge of Peace: God's Promise and Our Response," *Origins* 13, no. 1 (May 19, 1983). Hereinafter cited as Pastoral Letter with page number and column reference.

methods of employing force. There is little that needs to be said here about the justification for resorting to force. Whatever the earlier position taken toward the *jus ad bello*, in the twentieth century reconstruction of *bellum justum*, war is no longer a means generally permitted to states for the redress of rights that have been violated. Still less is war considered a legitimate means for changing the status quo. Armed force remains a means permitted to states only as a measure of self-defense against unjust attack. This is also the position taken in the bishops' letter and it echoes the earlier position taken in 1964 by the second Vatican Council. The Council declared: "As long as the danger of war persists and there is no international authority with the necessary competence and power, governments cannot be denied the right of lawful self-defense, once all peace efforts have failed."[5]

This restriction of the right of recourse to war is a far-reaching change from the classic doctrine, though how far-reaching is dependent upon the scope and meaning accorded to legitimate self-defense. In the classic doctrine, the just war was a war of execution, an act of vindicative justice, taken to punish an offending state for a wrong done and unamended. But the rights in defense of which the traditional doctrine permitted states to resort to war, in the absence of satisfactory alternative means of redress, were not restricted to the right of self-defense. The "blameless self-defense" of the classic doctrine represented only one cause justifying the resort to war, and a cause the justice of which appeared so self-evident to the expositors of the doctrine as scarcely to warrant discussion. The primary concern was with the problem of "aggressive" or offensive war (in the sense of the initiation of force). The broad response was simply that aggressive war was justified when undertaken by con-stituted authority, with right intention and as a last resort, to restore the order of justice violated by the offending state.

The classic doctrine was defensive then, in the sense that war was to be undertaken in defense of justice. It was not neces-

---

5. Second Vatican Council, *Pastoral Constitution on the Church in the Modern World*, December 7, 1965, n.c.: National Catholic Welfare Conference, 1966. The statement on war appears in part II, chap. 5.

sarily defensive in any other sense. War might be initiated to redress an injury, enforce one's rights, or forestall injurious action. A just war might thus comprise a preventive war. Not so today. In the twentieth-century reconstruction of *bellum justum*, the restriction of the just war to the war of self-defense rests on the presumption—indeed, conviction—that war no longer serves as an apt and proportionate means for resolving international conflicts. There are dissenters from this reconstruction of the classic doctrine. In the absence of a society possessed of effective collective procedures for protecting the rights of its members as well as for changing conditions that have become oppressive and inequitable, it is argued that the attempt to deny states this ultimate means of self-redress—save as a measure of self-defense against attack—is bound to fail. Nor is it clear, this argument persists, that the attempt to proscribe "aggressive" war ought to succeed—and this despite the destructiveness of war in this century—so long as these conditions persist that have always marked international society. Whatever the merits of this view, and it is not to be dismissed lightly, the dominant position today is that armed force is forbidden save as a measure of legitimate self-defense.[6]

How do current versions of *bellum justum* circumscribe this one remaining course justifying war? In fact, they seem to have little to say about the meaning and scope of legitimate self-defense. What they do have to say does not differ substantially from the more extended and detailed juristic analyses of the right of self-defense. The same difficulties and ambiguities marking the latter also mark the former. In both, uncertainty and controversy persist over the rights on behalf of which and the acts in response to which forcible measures of self-defense may be taken. The principal reason for this uncertainty and controversy are clear enough. While force may be forbidden to states, whether as a means for effecting change or as a means for protecting established rights, no viable and effective alternative to the institution of forcible self-help may exist. In these circumstances, the scope of the right of self-defense may largely deter-

---

6. The most persuasive presentation of the above view may be found in the various works of Julius Stone. See in particular, *Aggression and World Order* (Berkeley: University of California Press, 1958).

mine the degree of security states enjoy, since a right of self-redress that nevertheless forbids the threat or use of force may prove insufficient to the task of preserving many interests on which the security of states rest. Thus the endless controversies attending interpretations of critical provisions of the United Nations Charter, controversies that are echoed in the disparate interpretations given self-defense in current versions of *bellum justum*.

It is not primarily here that *bellum justum* today confronts reason of state, but rather in the restraints placed on the means or conduct of war. The general nature of that conflict is clear enough. Whereas reason of state must reject the claim that there are any inherent limits on the means that may be threatened or employed on behalf of the state, *bellum justum* must insist that there are such limits and that they may never be transgressed, whatever the circumstances. The argument of necessity must reject the claim of inherent limits on the means of war, not because it is informed by an "ethic of responsibility" requiring the statesman to calculate and to weigh the possible consequences of alternative courses of action, but because it presupposes as an ultimate end the preservation and continuity of the state. To this end, all else, if necessary, must be subordinated. *Bellum justum* evidently cannot share this presupposition, else it could not insist there are means that may never be employed. There is no denial here of the need to calculate and to weigh, but simply the insistence that whatever the results of calculation, certain limits must be imposed on the means permitted the statesman, limits that may never be transgressed. *Bellum justum* has a distinctive quality in that it is an "ethic of ultimate means."[7]

This quality is lost if the problem of means is reduced to

---

7. The term "ethic of responsibility" is taken from Max Weber's classic essay, "Politics as a Vocation." See H. H. Gerth and C. Wright Mills, ed., *Max Weber: Essays in Sociology* (New York: Oxford University Press, 1958), pp. 77 ff. Weber contrasts an "ethic of responsibility" with an "ethic of ultimate ends," the former being identified with the statesman and the latter with the Christian. One might just as reasonably, though, identify his ethic of responsibility with an ethic of ultimate ends, and his ethic of ultimate ends with an ethic of ultimate means. That, at any rate, is the position taken here for reasons elaborated in the text.

what is, in effect, another form of calculation. It is not enough to argue that one may never do evil so that good may come because the good will not come (only the evil), or that the evil act will corrupt the actor and thereby defeat his ends (however desirable in themselves), or that the means cannot be separated from the ends but are themselves the ends in the very process of coming into existence. Each of these familiar contentions is open to question. If this were not the case, if these contentions were instead beyond question, the task of the moralist would be greatly simplified. Certain means might then be absolutely forbidden not only because they are in and of themselves evil but also because they are imprudent, a form of mistaken calculation.

Experience shows, however, that good may come of evil, that the use of evil means does not always corrupt the actor, and that it is too simple to conceive of means as themselves the ends of action in the very process of coming into existence. If certain means are to be absolutely forbidden, they must be so forbidden because of their intrinsic evil. If one may never do evil that good may come, it is not because the good probably will not come but simply because one may never do evil.[8]

What are the restraints on means that may never be transgressed? In the conduct of war there is only one, but it is all-important. It is the principle forbidding the direct and intentional attack on noncombatants. The distinction between those who may be made the object of attack and those who may not be so made is held in *bellum justum* to define the essential difference between war and murder—between the permitted and the forbidden taking of human life. It is the deliberate killing of the innocent that is always to be avoided, that may never be justified even as a measure of reprisal taken in response to similar measures of an adversary. This is, in substance, the evil that may never be done or threatened, whatever the good that may be thought to come. In Vatican Council II indiscriminate warfare

---

8. The maxim "let justice be done though the heavens fall" aptly characterizes this position as does the saying "The Christian does rightly and leaves the result with the Lord." How could this ethic be what it pretends, though, if there is assurance that, after all, the heavens will not fall and that, in the end, the Lord will insure good results? Do we have here, despite pretentions to the contrary, simply a higher form of prudence, a more complex kind of calculation?

is condemned in these terms (terms that are repeated in the bishops' letter):

> Any act of war aimed indiscriminately at the destruction of entire cities or of extensive areas along with their population is a crime against God and man himself. It merits unequivocal and un-hesitating condemnation.[9]

This condemnation of indiscriminate warfare is, in effect, the condemnation of total war. Almost by definition, total war must prove indiscriminate in its conduct. Total war is also very likely to violate the other general principle regulating the conduct of war, the principle of proportionality. The norm requiring that the values preserved through force must be proportionate to the values sacrificed through force, is no more than a counsel of prudence. It expresses the common sense of the matter. When war becomes disproportionately destructive to the good it serves, it must be condemned. The judgements of proportionality, and its converse, are necessarily very rough and subject to considerable uncertainty and controversy. Still, they are indispensable to make if war is to be (anything close to) a rational and moral activity.[10]

---

9. Pastoral Letter, p. 15, col. I.

10. The criticism is regularly made that the principle of proportionality cannot impose meaningful constraints on the conduct of war. Devoid entirely of the element of specificity, invoked to weigh and to compare values that are incommensurable, it can be and has been employed to justify the most varied of actions. Moreover, experience shows that in war there is nearly always a temptation for the participants to assume a meaningful, even a necessary, relation between the measures they take and the purposes they entertain. Indeed, the deep-rooted need to justify force may be seen as driving men to draw this relationship, while the principle of proportionality provides them with the intellectual rationalization for doing so. In the attempts that have been made to justify nuclear war—virtually any *likely* nuclear war—in terms of proportionality, it is argued that we see the *reductio ad absurdum* of a principle that, in reality, has always been useless as a constraint on men's behavior.

The force of this criticism—one that I have shared—can scarcely be gain-said. Still, does not the denial of proportionality also lead to absurdity? Is it in fact possible even to consider the justice—or lack thereof—of war without considering at some point and in some manner the principle of proportionality? How else would we reach a *full* judgement on war and its conduct?

The principles of discrimination and proportionality determine, by and large, the justice of warfare. We have here, it need hardly be said, a rough and minimal justice, a *grenzmoral* as John Courtney Murray once observed.[11] Still, these principles are critical if war is to be even a barely tolerable activity. Of the two, it is the principle of discrimination that is much the more significant in the sense that it poses the clearer obstacle to, and stands in more apparent conflict with, the state and its necessities. It is of course the case that difficulty and uncertainty also attend application of the principle of discrimination. In forbidding the deliberate attack upon the innocent (civilian) population, we must still determine who are the innocent and what constitutes a deliberate attack upon them. The latter determination, particularly, has often been attended by considerable difficulties. These difficulties continue to lend themselves today, as they have lent themselves in the past, to manipulation by the state. Even so, if the principle of discrimination is not to be all but abandoned in practice, there is a point beyond which the line must be fairly clearly drawn between the demands of that principle and the necessities of the state. If conventional warfare in this century has already made increasingly imperative the drawing of this line, the prospect of nuclear warfare must make it many times more urgent.

Do nuclear weapons and the prospects held out by nuclear war invalidate reason of state? If the answer is that they do, there is no need to go beyond this question and to ask whether the use of nuclear weapons may be reconciled with the requirements of *bellum justum.* If the use of nuclear weapons holds out the likely prospect of destroying the state along with those values the state is supposed to protect, nuclear war represents the very antithesis of the idea of the state's *ratio.* This ancient justification of power is now at last turned against itself, as it were, by

---

11. John Courtney Murray, "Morality and Modern War," *The Church Peace Union* (1959), p. 5.

weapons that represent hypertrophy of power. This being so, the question of fulfilling the requirements of *bellum justum* can be no more than rhetorical.

Of course, whether the prospects held out by nuclear war— virtually any nuclear war—do invalidate reason of state and are irreconcilable with even the barest requirements of a just war depends on the character of such a conflict. But we are almost as much in the dark today about this as we have always been. After more than a generation of speculation and debate we cannot say with assurance what a nuclear war would be like and, above all, whether it might be subject to meaningful limitation. We do not know and cannot know short of the event itself whether a "central" war between the United States and the Soviet Union might be limited in any meaningful way. Nor do we or can we know short of the event itself whether the theatre use of nuclear weapons in the central front in Europe might be kept from spreading to much of the rest of the continent and, eventually, engulfing the homelands of the nuclear superpowers.

Our persisting ignorance in these matters must be asserted despite those who seem to know what a nuclear war, any and all nuclear war, would be like. No one knows or can know what remains and, let us hope, will continue to remain, unknowable. What we do know is that nuclear weapons are terribly destructive and that their rate of destructiveness leaves almost no time for second thoughts. We also know that our abiilty to cope with the demands imposed by nuclear war will be put, under the best of circumstances, to the most severe strain. Thus we have strong reason for believing, even if we cannot quite know, that virtually any war fought with the nuclear weapons we now have would prove very difficult to control and would involve, at the very least, casualties in the several millions on each side.[12] This is a very modest statement. Many would find it modest to the point of being quite misleading. Even so, on a matter that has invited and continues to invite almost unparalleled hyperbole, a little understatement can do no great harm.

---

12. The emphasis on weapons "we now have" is to distinguish them from weapons of great accuracy we may well have in the years ahead. Cf. infra. pp. 79.

It is not necessary to postulate the end of humanity in order to conclude that the use of nuclear weapons invalidates reason of state and is irreconcilable with the requirements of *bellum justum*, or any reasonable variation of that doctrine. Nor, for that matter, is it necessary to postulate a nuclear war resulting in hundreds of millions of casualties in order to reach these conclusions. Often in thinking about nuclear war our political and moral calculus has simply run amok. It has been inflated to the point of absurdity. The political and moral justification of nuclear war fails by applying far more modest standards than these. If it can be shown that a nuclear war is likely to destroy the end(s) for which it is waged, it can have neither political nor moral justification. If a nuclear war, though limited to Western Europe, is likely to result in the destruction of the countries in which it is waged, and presumably for the defense of which it is waged, it is difficult to find its political or moral justification. If a nuclear war, involving the territories of the two superpowers, results in the kind of devastation that makes impossible the retention of democratic processes and values, the war can have neither political nor moral justification. This may be said quite apart from any direct consideration of the manner in which the war is conducted, though the consequences of the war would themselves strongly suggest that the means of conducting it afford an independent ground for moral condemnation.

May one make the very uncertainty—the persisting uncertainty—attending the conduct and consequences of nuclear war a principal reason for denying moral justification to the use of nuclear weapons? Recently a notable effort has been made to do so. In the American Catholic bishops' letter, the uncertainties attending the use—any use—of nuclear weapons is given great emphasis. The bishops repeatedly express their "extreme skepticism" over whether a nuclear conflict could be controlled, however limited a manner in which it might begin. This skepticism over the prospects of limiting nuclear conflict in a way that could satisfy the requirements of political and moral rationality not only leads them to support a "no first use" position but to come very close to denying even the legitimacy of the retaliatory use of nuclear weapons in a limited exchange. For the conditions that the bishops insist must be answered satisfactorily before sanctioning any use of nuclear weapons cannot be answered satisfactorily. Indeed, these very conditions—which deal with various aspects of, and difficulties in, limiting the use of nuclear weapons—are largely what the nuclear debate has always been about. In demanding assurance that these conditions can be met and in insisting that the burden of proof rests with those who assert that meaningful limitation is possible, the bishops have taken a position that is the functional equivalent of one of denial.

Thus the result of placing the emphasis the bishops do on the issue of control is to come virtually to the position of condemning any and all use of nuclear weapons. The bishops do not directly and unequivocally support this conclusion. They do not say that the use of nuclear weapons—any and all use of nuclear weapons—is evil. But this is surely the central thrust of their message and it would be disingenuous to contend otherwise. The possibility is conceded that nuclear weapons might be used in morally permissible ways. But this possibility cannot be viewed as having any real significance in affecting the bishops' assessment. It cannot for the reason that the conditions indispensable to the use of nuclear weapons, according to the bishops, are—to repeat—conditions that cannot be fulfilled. The possibility the bishops concede is, accordingly, little more than theoretical; it is without significance for the altogether likely uses of nuclear weapons now and in the immediate future. These altogether likely uses prompt the bishops to conclude, that "to cross the nuclear threshold is to enter a world where we have no experience of control, much testimony against its possibility, and therefore no moral justification for submitting the human community to this risk."[13]

Even if we do not consider this argument as conclusive, it is still a very persuasive one. There is no morality in statecraft without prudence. But how is one to be prudent in the use of nuclear weapons? At the very least, prudence would seem to require an experience and knowledge about the use of nuclear weapons that we do not have. In this respect, it is useful to contrast the use of nuclear weapons with the threat to use them.

---

13. Pastoral Letter, p. 16, col. I.

We do have an experience, an ever growing experience, with deterrence. Here, there is reason to expect that prudent behavior can be maintained by both sides. For both sides have already behaved quite prudently for nearly three decades. This is no guarantee of the future, as critics of deterrence insistently point out. But it is at least a substantial reason for believing that deterrence may prove a manageable arrangement for an indefinite period ahead. Nuclear deterrence, it may then be argued, is compatible with prudence. By contrast, nuclear war would in all likelihood put prudence to an unbearable test. This is not the ringing moral condemnation of nuclear weapons that we have of late increasingly become accustomed to hearing. It is not such because it does not spring from the assumption—held to by many as an article of faith—that the use of nuclear weapons on however limited a scale must eventuate in the unlimited use of these weapons.

It is deterrence rather than nuclear war that expresses today the spirit of reason of state, just as it is deterrence rather than nuclear war that raises the more significant—certainly the more immediate—moral issues. Nuclear war is a recurrent nightmare that we hope will never materialize. Deterrence is part of our daily existence, even if it is an unseen part. The same air of unreality that attaches to speculation over how a nuclear war might arise and the character it would have, also attaches to the moral considerations attending the use of nuclear weapons. Do the moral judgements we may make on nuclear war really matter, however, save to moralists and a few kindred souls? More pointedly, perhaps, do these judgements really matter much save as they bear on what undoubtedly does matter: deterrence?

The first and, indeed, the last thing that needs to be said in any moral assessment of deterrence, is that it should not be regarded as a temporary arrangement. Deterrence should not be seen as a mere way station on the road, even if a long road, to a world without nuclear weapons. In retrospect, deterrence may one day be seen as just that. But its justification now cannot be made to turn on a prospect that from the vantage point of the present must appear as near utopian. It is true that the alternative to this proposition seems grim, since a world that is condemned to rely indefinitely on deterrence is a world that seems to have a permanent sentence of death hanging over it. Deterrence is merely a social contrivance and as such it is fallible. This being so, time must appear as the great nemesis, as we are constantly reminded. Over time, the familiar argument runs, the odds lengthen that deterrence will break down.

There is no really satisfactory response that may be made to this argument. The American bishops echo a rather general sentiment when, in giving their "strictly conditioned moral acceptance" to deterrence, they urge that deterrence "should be used as a step on the way toward progressive disarmament."[14] An arrangement that is only barely sanctioned morally must be marked by this corrective or redeeming process (progressive disarmament) if it is to be given continued approval. But the more specific measures the bishops propose in support of progressive disarmament would not achieve a nuclear-free world even if they were carried out. At best, what they would do is freeze the nuclear strategic status quo and make it marginally safer. To do that would not be an insignificant achievement. At the same time, it would not alter in any fundamental way the present structure of deterrence. Even Jonathan Schell's plan for "abolishing" nuclear weapons would not in fact do this, allowing as it does for the resurrection of deterrence in a very brief period should the political conditions requisite for abolition and its maintenance once break down.[15]

---

14. Pastoral Letter, p. 18, cols. II, III. In this the bishops follow previous utterances of the Catholic hierarchy that go back to the 1960s.

15. Jonathan Schell, *The Abolition*. In Schell's plan the once nuclear powers might always rearm with nuclear weapons. Deterrence structures might be resurrected and nuclear wars fought. The virtue of Schell's scheme, according to its author, is that if the abolition of nuclear weapons could once be effected, nuclear war would be no closer than two months, whereas now it is presumably only seven minutes away. In reality nuclear war today is normally six weeks to two months away, since that is the approximate time for a great crisis to appear and mature. The seven minutes nuclear war from out of the blue is, purely accidental nuclear war apart, a figment of fevered imaginations.

Nuclear weapons present us with a danger for which there simply is at present no apparently feasible way out. There are, of course, "ways out" that are no more than speculative. One can imagine a world in which all conflicts among states are resolved by methods other than war. Visions of a world in which force no longer plays the role it has always played require us to assume either that force can no longer secure the ends men desire or that men no longer desire the ends that have led them to employ force. Despite the expectations of some, the day that war will have lost its utility appears almost as distant as ever. So does the prospect of men's moral transformation.

Equally speculative is the way out that requires the transformation of the system rather than of man. Such transformation is not to be identified with a world that has succeeded in abolishing nuclear weapons, or, for that matter, conventional weapons as well. In a disarmed world, though still one consisting of sovereign states, the threat of force would persist as an instrument of diplomacy. It would do so because in the absence of effective supranational institutions, states could always break the disarmament agreement and rearm. War would remain the *ultima ratio* of diplomacy, though at one stage removed.

A world that no longer lives in the shadow of the nuclear threat must therefore be one presided over by a centralized authority. The functions this authority would have to perform have often been described as limited, because confined to the purpose of preventing war. But the structures and powers required for the prevention of armed conflict form the essential attributes of governance. The supranational authority would be charged with maintaining peace, insuring security, and providing for peaceful change. These are the principal functions of the state everywhere, although they are not performed with equal effectiveness everywhere. In the imagined case, these functions would have to be performed for a global society still comprised of nation-states, still divided by deeply antagonistic political and social systems, still marked by great disparities in development and still beset by hegemonic rivalries.

The prospects for transcending the nuclear threat through what Raymond Aron once termed a "conversion of history" may be set aside as utopian. Must the same be said for the prospects of escaping the world of deterrence through the agency that brought us into this world? The hope has grown that technology will yet deliver us from the nuclear evil, that having for long shown its malevolent side it will at last show its benevolent side. A familiar expression of this hope is found in the belief that for every offensive weapon there is an effective defense.

Unfortunately, experience does not bear out this optimism. It does not show that offensive weapons have regularly evoked offsetting defensive systems. What it does show, on balance, is that the best defense against offensive weapons is the same weapons used for defensive purposes. Nuclear weapons appear to confirm this experience, though they do so by carrying it a giant step further. Rather than actively to defend against the use of nuclear weapons, they passively defend by deterring the use of these weapons altogether.

The vision of transcending the world of deterrence through technology rests on the prospect of achieving the means to defend actively against the use of nuclear weapons, however these weapons are conveyed. Moreover, given the destructiveness of nuclear weapons, the means must be virtually perfect in their effectiveness. Anything that falls short of virtual perfection may strengthen, and markedly so, the stability of deterrence. Still, the improvement of deterrence is not to be confused with its transcendence. Technology may hold out the prospect of restoring faith in deterrence. But the hope that it may eventually lead as well to a world beyond deterrence corresponds to nothing in our past experience. Technology seems no more likely a candidate for delivering us from the world of deterrence than those transformations that are rightly regarded as utopian.

Nevertheless, there is a way out of the world of deterrence if one is willing to pay the price and to brave the consequences of this way. Pacifism remains today, as in the past, a way out. It is a way out because it does not depend upon the behavior of others. Pacifism is a unilateral way out of the world of deterrence because it is a unilateral way out of the world of statecraft in general. The same must be said of "nuclear pacifism," so long as it is understood that "nuclear" serves here as no more than a pleonasm. This is, however, not the common understanding, and certainly not the understanding of many who view with increasing favor the renunciation of nuclear weapons. The illusion persists that this nation might unilaterally renounce the use or the threat of nuclear weapons, and divest itself of these weapons, yet continue to resist an adversary that remains armed with them. To resist with weapons other than nuclear, though, would only risk annihilation at the hands of the adversary. If nuclear weapons are once abandoned, an elementary prudence must dictate the abandonment of conventional weapons as well.

Pacifism, nuclear or otherwise, is not simply another form of statecraft. Very nearly the same must be said of that modern variant of pacifism, nonviolent resistance. At one with traditional pacifism in renouncing war, the advocacy of nonviolence has frequently been marked by the refusal to draw the consequences from this renunciation pacifists have regularly drawn. Instead, nonviolence has been represented as a new kind of statecraft and, in the nuclear age, the only realistic statecraft.

Whatever the merits of nonviolence as a strategy the materially weak have employed against the strong, the experience of nonviolence appears to have almost no relevance to international conflict. Nonviolence is not a strategy for preserving the state's independence. Indeed, it can scarcely become a meaningful strategy until political independence has been lost. There is no reason to believe that the choice of nonviolent resistance will entail any lower price than that entailed by traditional pacifism. In both cases, it is not only the means but most of the ends of statecraft that must be abandoned.

Apart from submission, then, there are no apparently feasible ways out of the dangers imposed by deterrence. These dangers may perhaps be markedly moderated by technology, just as they may be moderated by politics. Nevertheless, any basic change in the deterrence relationship is unlikely to result from these developments. Deterrence, it appears, will remain a part of our "condition" for as far as we can presently see.

It is this very prospect that some find morally intolerable. Even if the risk of deterrence breaking down is considered to be quite low, the risks run are still intolerably high given the possible consequences of nuclear war. Jonathan Schell has put the case thus:

> Once we learn that a holocaust *might* lead to extinction we have no right to gamble, because if we lose, the game will be over, and

neither we nor anyone else will ever get another chance. There-fore, although, scientifically speaking, there is all the difference in the world between the mere possibility that holocaust will bring about extinction and the certainty of it, morally they are the same, and we have no choice but to address the issue of nuclear weapons as though we knew for a certainty that their use would put an end to our species.[16]

Schell's argument is simply that when infinity is multiplied by however small a fraction it still represents infinity. The extinc-tion of the species is taken to represent moral infinity (or rather immoral infinity). However slight the risk of nuclear war occur-ring and however slight the risk such war might lead to extinc-tion should it occur, when these risks are multiplied by infinity the result is still infinity. The uncertainties of deterrence must therefore be treated as a certainty and deterrence must be judged morally intolerable.

Even if this argument persuaded entirely there would re-main the problem of a viable alternative to an arrangement judged morally intolerable. The case Schell puts for the abolition of nuclear weapons requires as a precondition a political envi-ronment we do not have today, have never had, and are al-together unlikely to have in the future. This consideration apart, there is the difficulty with Schell's argument that it is not the only use that may be made of infinity in relation to deterrence. Suppose that, instead, we take the effectiveness of deterrence to be the product of the potential destructiveness of nuclear war and the (fractional) risk of deterrence breaking down. If we as-sume that the potential destructiveness of nuclear war equals infinity (i.e., extinction), then the effectiveness of deterrence is the product of infinity and some fraction. In this case, though, the effectiveness of deterrence is infinity and we have little to worry about.[17]

These "equations of infinity" are not new. Like virtually

---

16. Jonathan Schell, *The Fate of the Earth* (New York: Alfred A. Knopf, 1982), p. 95.

17. At least, little to worry over in the sense of a war that is due to human agency and not technological error or breakdown. There is increasing consensus among experts that if deterrence were ever to break down, it would not do so by virtue of technological cause.

everything else that has been said in the contemporary nuclear debate, variations of these arguments appeared a generation ago. What they established then, they also establish today. Nuclear deterrence lends itself to seemingly "infinite" manner and form of paradox.

The principal moral issue deterrence raises is whether one may threaten what would be evil to do. This is of course not the only issue raised by deterrence. Even if the moralist concludes that in this instance the threat to do evil is morally tolerable, he may also be expected to conclude that deterrence represents an extreme, or limiting, case. As such, it is a condition that must be made as effective as possible. Still, the prospect that the condition of deterrence may fail is one that cannot be excluded. This being so there is a duty to limit the evil wrought by nuclear war, as far as this is possible. These imperatives, as we know, are not easy to give meaning to in practice. They have provoked bitter and continuing controversy. Among many, perhaps most, the view persists that the two imperatives are and must remain mutually incompatible, that the effectiveness of deterrence rests largely on the conviction—and reality—of the impossibility of limiting the evil of nuclear war. It is particularly among those holding this view that there is an emphasis amounting to an obsession on the imperative to transcend the condition of deterrence, although the prospects for effecting such transcendence are, as already noted, negligible.

In asking whether one may threaten what would be evil to do, it is evidently assumed that the ends of the action are good. Were this not the case, no moral quandary would arise. One does arise only because of situations or circumstances in which there seems no alternative to threatening evil, and intending to do evil, that good may come. In the case of deterrence, what is the threat that it would be evil to carry out?

The answer will be apparent from the earlier discussion. Given the perspective of *bellum justum,* it is wicked to wage indiscriminate warfare, even in retaliation for acts of indiscriminate warfare. Equally from this perspective, a war that either destroys or does irreparable damage to the values in defense of which it is undertaken must be condemned. Years ago, Paul Tillich declared that nuclear war would be evil it it could not serve the principle of "creative justice." A war, Tillich wrote, that does not hold out "the possibility of a creative new beginning" because it "annihilates what it is supposed to defend" must be condemned.[18]

If discrimination and proportionality are accepted as the principal moral criteria by which justice in war is determined, what kind of nuclear deterrent, if any, would permit the solid prospect, if ever put to active use, of not doing evil? Evidently a deterrent that could be quite closely controlled, one that would permit us, in Albert Wohlstetter's words, "to hit what we aim at and only what we aim at."[19] The development of ever more accurate weapons opens up the prospect of a deterrent, nuclear and even conventional, that might be employed with considerable discrimination and within the broad limits of the principle of proportionality. The new technology of smart weapons promises a radical decrease in collateral damage, by permitting conventional weapons to replace nuclear weapons in many tasks, by dramatically raising the nuclear threshold and by diminishing the prospects of escalation.

The precision guided munitions do not and cannot free us from the great danger created by nuclear weapons. May they not, however, mitigate this danger by affording a greater opportunity to act in a more restrained and discriminate manner? Against the belief of some that they would have this effect, there is the conviction of others that they will be used to rehabilitate nuclear war. The new technology presumably will give rise to the illusion that nuclear weapons have at last been domesticated and are now virtually as usable as conventional weapons.

---

18. Paul Tillich, "The Nuclear Dilemma—A Discussion," *Christianity and Crisis* (November 13, 1961), p. 204. Tillich nevertheless justified deterrence, however destructive. His qualms were overcome by faith in deterrence—indeed, "existential" deterrence. "Practically," he wrote, "the very existence of atomic weapons on both sides is probably a sufficient deterrent."

19. Albert Wohlstetter, "Bishops, Statesmen, and Other Strategists on the Bombing of Innocents," *Commentary* (June 1983), pp. 15–35.

Once they are employed, however, the danger of escalation will inevitably arise. It is for these reasons that the American Catholic bishops take a dim view of the promise of the new technology. "The problem," the bishops declare, "is not simply one of producing highly accurate weapons that might minimize civilian casualties in any single explosion but one of increasing the likelihood of escalation at a level where many, even 'discriminating' weapons, would cumulatively kill large numbers of civilians."[20]

The bishops are of course right in insisting that while highly accurate weapons do not resolve the critical issue of limits, they may well prompt the illusion that this issue has now been resolved. Men have not been indiscriminate in war simply because they lacked the means to be discriminate. Discriminate means may be used in pursuit of immoderate ends. When they are, the means are very likely to be used indiscriminately. At the same time, this is an argument that may be employed against virtually any weapon. Indeed, in the end it is an argument against war itself, and certainly against war—whether nuclear or conventional—in the late twentieth century.

The precision guided weapons raise to a new level the persisting issue of the nuclear age between those who would seek safety in refusing to countenance almost any development that might have the effect of making nuclear war—or, for that matter, any war between the superpowers—more thinkable and those who are prepared to accept an incrementally greater risk of nuclear war in order to make its conduct less than apocalyptic. As a moral choice, it is difficult to see how this issue can be settled by an appeal to experience, although each side is constantly invoking history in support of its position. But history, as far as I can read it, does not seem to vindicate either position.

At any rate, the moral problem we presently face is not one of determining what kind of deterrent might be actively employed with the substantial prospect of not doing evil. Instead, it is one of deciding whether the deterrent we have today and are likely to have for some years allows the reasonable possibility of not doing evil. No one can answer this question with assurance. Still, to the extent we can answer it at all—and the effort must be made to do so—this answer appears to be nega-

---

20. Pastoral Letter, p. 18, col. I.

tive. Nor does it matter a great deal whether we are considering a direct strategic exchange between the nuclear superpowers or a nuclear conflict that is confined to Western Europe. In the former case, it is unlikely that either the United States or the Soviet Union would emerge as a viable entity. In the latter case, it is unlikely Western Europe, and particularly Germany, would do so.

It is of course possible to imagine a nuclear war in which this conclusion would not hold. But we must address the moral problem of deterrence not in terms of imaginable nuclear war but in terms of likely nuclear war. In this context, what matters is the kind of nuclear war the great nuclear powers are capable of waging and, so far as we know, have made plans to wage. If these plans include the attack and destruction of most major military targets in the adversary's homeland, and all indications are that this is the case, then the distinction that so much has been made of, between counterforce and countervalue targeting strategies, is of limited significance. The targeting plans of both sides are such that the resulting destruction will seem, by any reasonable application of established principles, both indiscriminate and disproportionate.

To this extent, it makes very little difference that the United States government declares its intention not to target civilian centers as such (or without "as such"). In the bishops' letter, government officials are cited as stating "that it is not U.S. strategic policy to target the Soviet civilian population as such or to use nuclear weapons deliberately for the purpose of destroying population centers."[21] Although the bishops were apparently satisfied that these statements met one moral criterion for assessing deterrence policy, the immunity of noncombatants from direct attack, they were anything but satisfied that the government's declared position responded to another moral problem, "namely, that an attack on military targets or militarily significant industrial targets could involve 'indirect' (i.e., unintended) but massive civilian casualties."[22] In turn, administration officials did little to assuage the bishops' doubts. On the

21. Pastoral Letter, p. 17, col. III. And administration sources cited in note 81.

22. Pastoral Letter, p. 18, col. I.

contrary, they are cited in the letter as "hoping" any nuclear war could be kept limited, but "prepared" to retaliate in a "massive" way if necessary. They also agreed that in a substantial exchange civilian casulty levels "would quickly become truly catastrophic" and that even if attacks were limited to military targets the resulting number of deaths "would be almost indistinguishable from what might occur if civilian centers had been deliberately and directly struck."[23]

The bishops conclude from these statements of the administration and from what is known of targeting plans that it is not enough to assert and even to have an intention not to strike civilians directly. However sincere that intention and however honest the efforts made to implement it, a nuclear war is still likely to be "morally disproportionate, even though not intentionally indiscriminate."[24] In this conclusion, one might almost suspect the bishops of a fine irony. Either that or they must be considered as seriously subscribing to the notion of the "intentless" destruction of entire societies. In truth, the prospect held out by nuclear war threatens to make of the issue of intent a grotesque parody.

If we are instead to preserve a sense of realism in these matters, we must acknowledge that the significance of intention decreases roughly as the destructiveness of war increases. There is no mystery in why this is so. As war becomes more and more destructive, the principle of proportionality must take on ever greater significance. At some extreme point, we must assume, that principle is clearly breached, and this quite apart from the interests at stake in the conflict. Nuclear war, we have strong reason to believe, represents that extreme point. It does so even if we continue to insist upon an intentionality that seems at complete odds with events in the objective order.

The threat upon which deterrence rests today is a threat to do evil despite a strategic policy that does not target the Soviet civilian population—or, at any rate, does not directly target the

---

23. Pastoral Letter, p. 18, col. I.
24. Pastoral Letter, p. 18, col. I.

Soviet civilian population. It is a threat to do evil whether or not it is regarded as intentionally indiscriminate. For the consequences of a nuclear war that goes beyond the most limited exchange are not only expected to go beyond any reasonable application of the principle of proportionality; they are also expected to be indistinguishable from a war in which the civilian population has been made the direct object of attack. Moreover, we must remind ourselves that this nation's strategic policy remains based today, as it has been based in the past, upon the threat of retaliating in kind to any one of several types of attack by the Soviet Union. This threat of retaliation is evidently a conditional threat to do evil if driven to it. The threat of retaliation that constitutes the foundation of deterrence, and has done so from the outset, also expresses with a clarity that is as striking as it is depressing, the conflict between the requirements of *bellum justum* and the requirements of reason of state.

Nevertheless, efforts to effect a reconciliation of the two continue today, though they are no more successful than they were a generation ago. Almost invariably, these efforts have taken the form of drawing ingenuous distinctions in the case of deterrence between threat and intent as well as between different types of intent. Thus it has been argued that even if deterrent strategies rely on the threat to do evil, that threat still does not necessarily imply an actual intent to do evil. If what is evil to do must also be evil to intend to do, however small the chance that this intent will have to be carried out, it does not follow that what is evil to intend to do must also be evil to threaten to do. Deterrence structures may rest on a threat to do evil that still need not betray an intent to do evil. The moralist may question the justification of threatening to do evil, though not intending to do evil. Even so, there is a difference between a threat that carries no intent to act in the manner threatened and a threat that does so.

But all this argument succeeds in doing is to establish that a threat to act may be distinguished from an intent to act. It does not indicate how the threat on which deterrence is based can be effectively maintained without also maintaining the intent to carry out the threat if necessary. Nor does it indicate how, in practice, an intentless threat may be distinguished from an intentful threat without putting the threat to the one and only reliable test. In the absence of this test, it is true, the argument cannot be disproved. Still, it seems reasonable to assume that in the absence of persuasive evidence to the contrary a deterrent threat to do evil also implies an intent to do evil.

In addition to the distinction drawn between threat and intent, it has been urged that deterrence permits and even requires us to distinguish between an interim and a final or ultimate intention. On this view, there is no ultimate intention to do evil only an interim intention. Paradoxically, one's ultimate intention is salvaged morally by an interim intention about which there is no doubt. If my interim intention is clearly to do evil, and my adversary is left in no doubt, I will never have to do evil. My interim intent not only insures that intent will not have to be acted on; the knowledge of this presumably permits me ultimately not to intend to do evil at all. In one of the recent versions of this argument, Michael Novak writes: "Those who intend to prevent the use of nuclear weapons by maintaining a system of deterrence in readiness for use do *intend* to use such weapons, but only in order *not* to use them, and do *threaten* to use them but only in order to *deter* their use." The "fundamental moral intention in nuclear deterrence," Novak declares, "is never to have to use the deterrent force." Only a "secondary intention" to do so is necessary, since without that secondary intention a deterrent is but an "inert weapon backed up by a public lie."[25] Novak's argument is interesting only as an example of the lengths to which some moralists will go to reconcile the needs of deterrence with the requirements of moral principle— in this case, Catholic moral principle. The argument itself can scarcely be taken seriously, for it rests on an evident confusion of intent and hope. Although we intend to use the deterrent should certain circumstances ever arise, we hope they never will arise. Nevertheless, our hope rests on an intent to do evil.[26]

---

25. Michael Novak, "Moral Clarity in the Nuclear Age," *National Review* (April 1, 1983), pp. 382–84.

26. In a sweeping critique of Novak, J. M. Cameron points out: "The only version of the Novak doctrine we can hope to save is: We hope the deterrent will never be used, but this hope is vain unless we here and now have a strong and unwavering intention to use, in certain circumstances, nuclear weapons against the enemy." "Nuclear Catholicism," *The New York Review of Books* (December 22, 1983), p. 40.

Deterrence continues to rest today on the threat, and the intent, to do evil. Must it for this reason be condemned? Among Catholic moralists, at least, one might expect the condemnation of deterrence, since there is no apparent way that one can reconcile deterrent structures with the injunction against either doing or intending to do evil that good may come. Yet with few exceptions, these moralists have refrained from condemning deterrence. In this, they have but followed in the footsteps of the most authoritative voices of the Church.

Thus although the second Vatican Council in 1965 condemned indiscriminate warfare, it did not condemn structures of deterrence that rested, in the last resort, upon the threat of indiscriminate warfare. On the contrary, the most reasonable interpretation of the Council's position on the morality of deterrence is that the means that may never be employed and the evil that may never be done may nevertheless be threatened. While warning that the "method of deterrence" was "not a safe way to preserve a steady peace," the Council nevertheless approved of deterrence in stating: "Many regard this as the most effective way by which peace of a sort can be maintained between nations at the present time."

The subsequent declarations of Church authorities have been less acquiescent of deterrence. Still, they have stopped short of condemnation. In 1976, the American bishops stated that "not only is it wrong to attack civilian populations but it is also wrong to threaten to attack them as part of a strategy of deterrence."[27] Beginning with this statement, there is an injunction in all such declarations to follow that the attitude of the Church toward deterrence will be heavily, perhaps even decisively, influenced by the efforts of government to reduce, and ultimately to remove altogether, nuclear weapons. In 1979, Cardinal John Krol expressed a willingness to tolerate the possession of nuclear weapons for deterrence but only so long as there is hope of a "phasing out altogether of nuclear deterrence and

---

27. *To Live in Christ Jesus*, National Conference of Catholic Bishops (Washington, D.C.: U.S. Catholic Conference, 1976), p. 34. Cited in Pastoral Letter, p. 17, col. I.

the threat of mutual-assured destruction." Barring that hope, Cardinal Krol warned, "the moral attitude of the Catholic Church would certainly have to shift to one of uncompromising condemnation of both use and possession of such weapons."[28] A less emphatic, but essentially similar position toward deterrence was expressed by Pope John Paul II in 1982.[29]

It is the position taken by the American bishops in their 1983 letter, however, that has attracted a degree of attention and provoked an amount of comment and controversy that is virtually without precedent in these matters. What did the bishops have to say about nuclear war and particularly about deterrence that is so startling as to merit the attention it has thus far received?

In part, the answer is that the attention given the pastoral letter must be accounted for simply by the unusual circumstances in which it appeared—that is, the circumstances of an anti-nuclear weapons movement of unprecedented size and momentum. In part, however, the letter has attracted widespread attention because it has carried the efforts of predecessors a large step further. In so doing, it has come very close to condemning any and all use of nuclear weapons. The use of these weapons is rejected, whether they are employed against military targets or against civilian centers of population, whether in a first strike or a retaliatory second strike, whether in a strategic or theatre nuclear war. The condemnation of nuclear war is very nearly complete. Although the barest trace of ambiguity remains in the bishops' discussion of limited nuclear war, that is all that remains.

This near absolute condemnation of nuclear war cannot but have a bearing on the moral assessment of deterrence. If nuclear weapons are illegitimate because their use cannot be controlled or their effects limited, must not deterrence structures that rest on the threat to use these weapons also be in principle illegitimate? And does not the approval of such structures amount to

---

28. Cardinal John Krol, Testimony on Salt II, *Origins* (1979), p. 197. Cited in Pastoral Letter, p. 17, col. I.

29. John Paul II, *Message* U.N. Special Session, 1982:3. Cited in Pastoral Letter, p. 17, cols. I, II.

the intent, however conditional, to do evil that good may come? So it would seem.[30] But the rejection of nuclear war is one thing and the rejection of deterrence quite another. As the supreme expression of reason of state today, the rejection of deterrence is—or would be—a momentous step. The bishops do not take this step. Instead, they are led "to a strictly conditioned moral acceptance of nuclear deterrence." But what this conditionality amounts to is not altogether apparent in the light of the bishops' statement. Opposed to both "counter value" and "counter force" targeting, the bishops do not indicate the targeting plan in support of a deterrent strategy they would approve. What they do indicate is that the kind of deterrent sufficient to elicit their "conditioned" acceptance is one designed "only to prevent the use of nuclear weapons by others." Any proposals to go beyond this, they declare, "to planning for prolonged periods of repeated nuclear strikes and counterstrikes, or 'prevailing' in nuclear war, are not acceptable." It is, to use a familiar dichotomy, a purely war-deterring and not a war-fighting strategy that they find acceptable. For this reason as well, we read, " 'sufficiency' to deter is an adequate strategy; the quest for nuclear superiority must be rejected."[31]

What the bishops have done is to tie a moral theory to a particular view of deterrence. The principles governing the just conduct of war have been linked to a strategic doctrine. As between those who believe that deterrence follows very largely from the existence of nuclear weapons and those who believe a credible theory of use must be developed if deterrence is to be assured, the bishops have plainly decided for the first. Having done so, they have also endowed their chosen view with minimal moral acceptability while judging as morally unacceptable the alternative view.

---

30. Indeed, in their summary of the pastoral letter, the bishops declare: No use of nuclear weapons which would violate the principles of discrimination or proportionality may be *intended* in a strategy of deterrence. The moral demands of Catholic teaching require resolute willingness not to intend or to do evil even to save our own lives or the lives of those we love.

31. Pastoral Letter, p. 18, cols. I, II.

Although asserting that only one view of deterrence is morally acceptable, they have not persuasively demonstrated why this is so. Indeed, they often seem quite unaware that what they reject as morally unacceptable is also primarily a strategy for deterring nuclear war and not one for waging such a war. Moreover, the manner of deterrent to which the bishops do give their moral sanction is not at all clear from their "criteria." It is, for example, not enough to declare that "deterrence exists only to prevent the use of nuclear weapons by others." This only begs the question of adequacy; it does not answer it. For the great question is: what kind of deterrent is most effective in preventing the use of nuclear weapons by others? The bishops apparently think they have answered this question by the term "sufficiency." In fact, they have only found another way of phrasing the question.

Moreover, even if these questions were to be given clear answers, they would nevertheless leave unanswered the principal moral issue deterrence must raise for the bishops. Even if the bishops are taken to have endorsed the "ideal" deterrent, having done so would not afford a solution to the moral problem raised by deterrence. The ideal deterrent would be one that satisfies almost perfectly the requirements of effectiveness and stability. Still, the ideal deterrent, no less than other deterrents, would rest on the threat to do evil. In morally accepting it, however strictly conditioned their acceptance, the bishops necessarily accept as a means the threat to do evil.

Have the bishops in their "strictly conditioned moral acceptance" of deterrence nevertheless managed to eviscerate it? A number of critics so argue. "You may keep the weapons," Charles Krauthammer interprets the bishops as saying, "but you may not use them. In sum, the only moral nuclear policy is nuclear bluff." But deterrence, Krauthammer argues, "is not inherent in the weapons. It results from a combination of possession and the will to use them. If one side renounces, for moral or other reasons, the intent of ever actually using nuclear weapons, deterrence ceases to exist."[32]

32. Charles Krauthammer, "On Nuclear Morality," *Commentary*, (October 1983) p. 49.

This view goes too far in its rejection of "existential" deterrence. In some measure, deterrence *is* inherent in nuclear weapons and the fact of possessing them. There is, after all, some merit in doctrines of existential deterrence. Admittedly, the bishops have put existential deterrence to an exacting test by virtually renouncing any use of nuclear weapons while retaining possession of them. But it was only in this manner that they could attempt to effect a compromise between the demands of moral principle and the necessities of state.

It is another matter to ask whether this compromise may not have been made at the expense of both moral principle and necessity of state and that in trying to be as wise as serpents while as innocent as doves the bishops were neither.[33] One may sympathize entirely with the bishops' dilemma in trying to come to terms with deterrence and yet conclude that their almost heroic effort may not, in the end, serve either moral principle or state necessity. Surely, the effect of the bishops' efforts, and of similar efforts, must be, if persisted in, to weaken the credibility of the deterrent. For the renunciation of use they advocate *does* have consequences in a democratic society, and it is an illusion to believe otherwise. The bishops' effort must therefore increase the risk, however small the increase may be, of Soviet behavior that leads to the nuclear precipice. Is this increased risk the price of adhering to moral principle? One must doubt that it is. The bishops may not intend using nuclear weapons, but they do obviously intend that the Soviets remain uncertain about whether the weapons may not after all be used despite our firm renunciation of their use. Is this not, however, a case of entertaining a wrongful intent, only at one remove? If nuclear war and particularly deterrence raise novel and difficult moral issues, as the bishops insist, is it plausible to credit the solution of these issues by clever devices?

These remarks should not be misunderstood. The bishops

33. Cf. Francis X. Winters, S. J., "The American Bishops on Deterrence— 'Wise as Serpents: Innocent as Doves,'" *Science, Technology and Human Values* (Summer 1983), pp. 23–29, for the argument that the bishops successfully combined moral purity and political relevance. In tolerating the retention of the nuclear arsenal while urging a greater effort in conventional arms, Father Winters concludes that the bishops' effort might even enhance deterrence.

are not faulted here for taking the position that the likely prospects held out by nuclear war—almost any nuclear war—are
irreconcilable with the essential requirements of *bellum justum.*
They may go too far in assuming they know what a nuclear war
would be like. Still, it is difficult to contest the proposition that a
nuclear war of almost any kind that is likely to occur would
represent a gigantic leap into the unknown, and that the prospects of controlling it in any meaningful manner would be no
better than marginal. This proposition forms the bedrock of the
moral case against the use of nuclear weapons. The bishops
have made it central to their view and they were quite right to
have done so.

The bishops have been criticized for weakening deterrence.
This they have done. They have done so, in the first place, by
denying moral justification to the use of nuclear weapons in
virtually all of the circumstances these weapons are likely to be
used. Yet most of their critics have themselves carefully refrained from morally justifying the use of nuclear weapons. The
critics may have no doubts about the morality of deterrence. But
the morality of deterrence rests, after all, on the threat of nuclear
weapons, not their use. It is true that to carry maximum credibility, the threat needs to be backed up by the visible readiness and
the clear intent to use nuclear weapons. Still, the threat is not
the use. Faith in deterrence, we are reminded, rests largely upon
the belief that in the will to use nuclear weapons rests the assurance (or hope) of not having to use them. The greater the will,
the smaller the prospects of nuclear war.

The bishops have weakened this will, however incrementally, by denying moral justification to the use of nuclear
weapons. When this is said as a criticism of their effort, the
question fairly arises: what were they to do? One possible answer is that they might have instead given their moral approval
to nuclear war. (For that is what approving of the use of the
deterrent amounts to.) But this, with rare exception, even the
bishops' critics will not do. While taxing the bishops with having declared the use of nuclear weapons immoral, these critics
do not affirm the morality of using nuclear weapons in the circumstances in which they are likely to be used. The evident

implication is that the critics too are hard put to give moral sanction to the use of nuclear weapons.[34]

Alternatively, the bishops might simply have remained silent on the issue. One has the distinct impression that this is what most critics believe the bishops should have done. The real criticism of the letter, though seldom voiced, is that it is indiscrete in calling our attention once again to the moral issues raised by nuclear weapons. For the bishops to have remained silent on these issues, however, would have broken with the past and with what the hierarchy of the Chruch increasingly considers as its pastoral duty and vocation. Moreover, silence on so crucial an issue as this would be altogether inconsistent with taking a moral position on a host of less transcendent issues. In fact, the bishops had little choice but to pronounce themselves, if not sooner than later, on nuclear weapons. Nor was it possible, in doing so, to limit themselves to the issue of use, while leaving in abeyance the matter of threat. Since the threat rather than the use is the reality in which we daily find ourselves, such limitation would have been seen, and rightly so, as simple evasion.

It is the manner in which deterrence is addressed, and not the fact that deterrence is addressed, that must evoke criticism. Of the three paths that were in principle open to the bishops, they chose the one that attempted to reconcile the irreconcilable. In doing so, they have provided yet another demonstration that there is no way by which necessity of state—and certainly necessity of state in the nuclear age—can be reconciled with *bellum justum*. If the bishops were to remain faithful to the essential requirements of the latter, they had little alternative but to condemn deterrence.

They might, on the other hand, have taken the course of compromising, if not quite openly breaking with, their moral

34. Krauthammer, ("On Nuclear Morality") for example, nowhere gives his moral approval to nuclear war. What he approves of is deterrence. It is the lesser evil, or, as he puts it, deterrence is better than the alternative. Deterrence, he says, "has worked." This being so, "one is morally obliged to come up with a better alternative." Whatever one makes of these and similar statements, they are not a defense of the moral legitimacy of nuclear war.

tradition. This is what the French Catholic bishops appear to have done in their extraordinary statement on issues of war and peace in the nuclear age.[35] The only respect in which the French bishops are unwilling to confront without illusion the grim reality of the world of deterrence is in their reluctance to concede that this world is more than a very transient one and that structures of deterrence are more than a "momentary response" to its necessities. But this reluctance is understandable when one considers that in the French case deterrence openly rests, as the bishops acknowledge, on an anti-city strategy. Yet the bishops sanction "this mortal game at the doors of hell."

They do so, moreover, while fully reaffirming the position of Vatican Council II that an act of war directed to the indiscriminate destruction of civilian populations is a crime against God and man and is to be unequivocally condemned. But "threat is not use" they insist. It is not evident that "the immorality of use make[s] the threat immoral." A critical moral distinction is accordingly drawn between the evil of nuclear war and the evil of deterrence. "Faced with a choice between almost unstoppable evils, capitulation or counterthreat, one chooses the lesser without claiming to make a good of it."

The French bishops are quite aware of what they have done, when viewed from their own moral traditions, in accepting a strategy of deterrence as the lesser evil. Deterrence, they state in a note to their text, is "a proximate occasion of grave sin! . . . but a necessary occasion, as classic morals say." And they go on to declare: "Once more we come across an ethic of distress, which is acceptable only on condition that it be placed in a dynamic perspective, one of gradualness, of moving beyond and on condition of not making the lesser evil a good."

This "ethic of distress" represents the compromise, the placing in abeyance, of a moral tradition. In saying that what may not be done may nevertheless be threatened, the French bishops have evidently compromised the Pauline principle that evil is not to be done—or intended—that good may come of it. The American bishops had sought to justify deterrence in similar fashion in an earlier draft of their letter only to drop the argument of the lesser evil in the final version. They did so despite the fact that Vatican Council II, and subsequent declarations by the Church hierarchy, had justified the morality of deterrence by accepting the assumption that we may intend to do evil that good may come. Yet the American bishops have not in fact consistently rejected that assumption. Instead, what they have done is to accept it in disguised form.

The principal moral issue deterrence has raised from the outset seems no nearer resolution today. Why should this continue to trouble some? Why should it matter that the peace of deterrence ultimately rests on the threat, and the intent, to do evil? If the ends sought by deterrence are good, why should it not serve as the means to achieve that good, whatever the quality of the intention that may inform it?

One answer to these questions is simply that the intent to do evil is the precondition for doing evil. If one has an intent to do evil, the day may well come, and likely will come, when evil will be done. And even if it is not done, the entertaining of an intent to do evil must have an effect on the character of those who harbor such intent. The price of holding an evil intent is the moral deformation of the holder, a deformation that will eventually manifest itself in other and perhaps quite unexpected ways. Finally, we are told that unless there are absolute or categorical limits on the means permitted the statesman, the door is open to any and every evil.

In the case of deterrence, these considerations are invoked today as they were invoked a generation and more ago. Deterrence, it was said then, as it is said now, cannot go on indefinitely. Eventually, it must break down, and this probably sooner rather than later. In the early 1960s, as in the early 1980s, prophetic voices were heard to the effect that deterrence would not last out the decade. Yet the relationship of mutual deterrence between the Soviet Union and the United States is now well into its third decade. With one exception, the Cuban missile crisis, this relationship has not come close to the breaking point, and even with respect to the Cuban missile crisis it remains a matter of controversy how close the great nuclear powers came to the precipice.

The historical record of deterrence, such as it is, is not invoked to suggest that the future must prove to be as benign as the past. It may not be. Besides, everyone knows that the distinctive problem of the deterrence relationship is that one failure may prove fatal to the parties. But if the historical record cannot be viewed as a source of great comfort and reassurance, it also cannot be viewed as a source of despair. The deterrence relationship has been a learning experience on both sides. The degree of sophistication and—yes—wisdom in regard to deterrent structures is considerably greater in the 1980s than it was in the 1960s. Although deterrence rests today, as it rested yesterday, on the threat and intent to do evil, the prospects that evil will one day be done have not increased. If anything, they appear to have modestly diminished.

Nor, after a generation, is the evidence of moral deformation very impressive. In the earlier years of the age of deterrence, one moralist plaintively asked: "How can a nation live with its conscience and know that it is preparing to kill twenty million children in another nation if the worst should come to the worst?"[36] The same kind of question is still asked today, though now it should be quite apparent that a nation can without difficulty live with its conscience though its security is ultimately based on the threat to annihilate another nation.[37] It can

---

36. John C. Bennett, "Moral Urgencies in the Nuclear Context," in *Nuclear Weapons and the Conflict of Conscience,* ed. John C. Bennett (New York: Scribners, 1962), p. 101.

37. The purist will object that there is no such thing as a nation's conscience or a collective conscience. He is of course right. But there is such a thing as individual consciences that are manifested collectively and this is how the text should be understood.

Moralists find deterrence particularly offensive because it is based on hostage holding. Deterrence is based on the threat to deprive of their freedom (above all, their lives) persons who are quite innocent of any wrong doing. Entire populations are made responsible for the acts of those relatively few individuals who make up governments and over whom these populations may have little or no control. Yet the novelty of deterrence, here as elsewhere, is not

do so because the conscience of a nation is not as susceptible to moral deformation as is the conscience of individuals. What leads to the moral deformation of individuals need not do so in the case of nations. The cynic will tell us that the reason for this is that the moral sense of nations is congenitally deformed. Even if the cynic goes too far, there is little reason to question the considerable difference between the moral sensitivity of individuals and of nations.

Then, too, the relatively limited effect of deterrence on the collective psyche must be attributed in part to the nature of deterrent structures and the manner in which the deterrence relationship and the threat that sustains it are generally perceived. It has long been noted that by comparison with an earlier age the establishment required by deterrent structures is relatively unobtrusive in its physical presence. This quality of relative unobtrusiveness in the daily life of society, when coupled with the almost incalculable effects of employing nuclear weapons, conferred an esoteric character on deterrence from the outset.

It is this character that in large part accounts for the moral indifference attending the implications of deterrent strategies. It is the same character that also largely explains the marginal effects deterrent strategies appear to have had on the societies supporting them.

---

in instituting something heretofore unknown in interstate relations but in carrying an established feature of these relations to an extreme. The relations of nations have always been based on hostage holding, since these relations have always been based on the pattern of collective responsibility. War provides the great example of this pattern and, for this reason, has long offended moralists. Measures in war injurious to the innocent, Adam Smith wrote two centuries ago, "can by no means be founded on justice and equity, properly so called. . . . [They] must be founded upon necessity which, indeed, in this instance is a part of justice. . . . In war there must always be the greatest injustice, but it is inevitable." *Lectures on Justice, Police, Revenue and Arms*, ed. Edwin Cannon (1896). Quoted in Arnold Wolfers and Lawrence W. Martin, *The Anglo-American Tradition in Foreign Affairs* (New Haven: Yale University Press, 1956), p. 84. Smith's point is that it is in the very nature of war as a collective enterprise that the innocent must suffer along with the guilty. Analogously, we may say that it is in the very nature of deterrence as a collective enterprise that the innocent must be held hostage for the good behavior of their government. Again, what distinguishes deterrence is its quantitative dimensions.

There remains the view that unless there are absolute or categorical limits on the means permitted the statesman, the door is opened to any and every evil. Why this must be so, however, has never been quite clear. Even if the position is taken that there are no absolute limits on means, and that it is not possible to reconcile the necessities of statecraft—above all, of war—with the injunction that evil may not be done, there remain means and means, just as there is still evil and evil. If the issue that must be faced and somehow resolved is not whether one may do evil that good may come, but rather how much evil one may do that any good may come, it is not for this reason without significance. There is surely an important difference between destroying a city in order to destroy a military objective within or near it and destroying the military objective, although such destruction inevitably involves the deaths of noncombatants. Moreover, there is an important difference even though in both cases the death and injury to the innocent is a means to the desired end and even though in both cases the death and injury to the innocent are intended.

Although it is regularly set forth as a self-evident truth, the assumption that once we accept that evil must be done in war any behavior is sanctioned is no more compelling than the assumption that if we only believe evil may never be done our behavior will thereby be restrained. Instead of restraining our behavior, the belief that evil may never be done may only strain our ingenuity. If evil may never be done, the practical import of this injunction will still depend on the manner in which doing evil is conceived. Given sufficient ingenuity of conception, war takes on the character of an event in which ever greater evil effects may result yet apparently through no evil acts.

These considerations may be pushed too far. Clearly, in some sense it is the case that even for collectives the intent to do evil is the precondition for doing evil, that the price for holding an evil intent is the moral deformation of the holder, and that to acknowledge that evil must be done is to open the door to any and every evil. But the questions persist: in what sense is this the case? And what is the alternative to deterrence, with its threat to do evil? Surely it makes a difference for moral judgement if one assesses the prospects for deterrence breaking down as something close to infinitesimal and the debilitating effects of the deterrent threat as no more than marginal. In this case we are left with the argument that an act which would be unjust to commit ought never to be threatened, however remote the contingency that the act will ever be committed and whatever the consequences that may follow if the threat is abandoned (and, in contrast to the position taken by the bishops, the abandonment of the deterrent threat is persuasively conveyed to the adversary through measures of unilateral disarmament). When reduced to this pure form, the argument seems singularly unpersuasive. One may question whether the moralists themselves are consistently prepared to accept it.

Even if the prospect that deterrence might fail is acknowledged as a not too finite possibility there remains the question: what is the alternative to deterrence with its threat to do evil? Obviously, the one clear alternative, in principle, is the abandonment of the means heretofore distinctive to a strategy of nuclear deterrence in particular *and* to statecraft in general. It is not unilateral nuclear abnegation that constitutes a viable alternative but pacifism as it is traditionally understood. To confront an adversary who remains in possession of nuclear weapons with conventional weapons is only to raise the distinct prospect of eventual annihilation. George Kennan may now believe that nuclear weapons are useful only for frightening people with weak nerves. But the answer to Kennan is that the world is, and has always been, full of people with weak nerves. Besides, it scarcely requires weak nerves to fear nuclear weapons when they are possessed only by an adversary. All that is required is a sane respect for the most destructive force man has yet been able to extract from nature.

DETERRENCE AND THE LAPSE OF FAITH
The Nuclear Debate I

In RETROSPECT, what seems remarkable about the nuclear debate that arose in the 1980s, is that for virtually a generation the issue of nuclear weapons had not been of central concern in public life. It had not been so despite the fact that during these years the Soviet Union had transformed the nature of the strategic balance. It had not been so despite the technological changes that had been made in nuclear weaponry, changes that might have been expected to have awakened sharply and widespread anxiety over the stability of the strategic balance. Finally, it had not been so even on the one occasion, in the course of the 1973 Mideast War, when in response to what was perceived by the American government as a serious threat by the Soviet Union to intervene in that conflict, American strategic forces were moved to an alert condition. Certainly, the years between the Cuban missile crisis and the Soviet Union's invasion of Afghanistan had not been without portentous developments in the sphere that provokes so much anxiety today. Yet these developments did not begin to provoke a comparable anxiety.

In one view, a heightened sensitivity today to the dangers of nuclear weapons reflects the heightened perils of the competition in arms or the "arms race." In the 1983 pastoral letter of the American Catholic bishops, we read that "the dynamic of the arms race has intensified" and that one compelling reason for the letter is the growing dangers this dynamic holds out.[1] The nuclear freeze movement has been largely predicated on the belief that the danger of nuclear war in the late 1980s and 1990s will be greater than ever before because of weapons systems that, in the words of a movement leader, "will increase the pressure on both sides to use their nuclear weapons in a crisis, rather than risk losing them in a first strike."[2] The *New York Times* national security correspondent expresses the growing concern that: "In 10 to 15 years, new technologies now being developed and tested could, if deployed, fundamentally and irretrievably undermine the basic philosophy that has been the center of both sides' nuclear strategy—mutual deterrence."[3] These technological developments could make nuclear war "seriously thinkable for the first time."[4]

This view is addressed more to the future than to the present. Yet it is also relevant to the present, for a dangerous future

1. "The Challenge of Peace: God's Promise and Our Response," *Origins,* May 19, 1983, p. 1.

2. Randall Forsberg, "Call to Halt the Nuclear Arms Race" in *Seeds of Promise: The First Real Hearings on the Nuclear Arms Freeze,* Randall Forsberg et al. (Andover, Massachusetts: Brick House Publishing, 1983), p. 197.

3. Leslie H. Gelb, "Is the Nuclear Threat Manageable?" *The New York Times Magazine,* March 4, 1984, p. 26.

4. To similar effect, McGeorge Bundy, "Atomic Diplomacy Reconsidered," *Bulletin: The American Academy of Arts and Sciences* (October 1984), pp. 25–44. In speculating on why we were "relatively comfortable about nuclear weapons" in the years between the Cuban missile crisis and the late 1970s, Bundy finds the principal reason in our confidence in the stability of the strategic balance. This confidence he believes, did not come primarily from the relationship of détente that characterized those years but from our conviction "that no one on either side, in or out of uniform, in or out of a moment of crisis, could ever suppose for one moment that there was anything to be gained—or indeed any prospect of anything but self-inflicted catastrophe—in any appeal to the arbitrament of general war." The erosion of this confidence is attributed mainly to the changes that have been made in recent years in the weapons systems themselves. Alarmed by the advent of large accurate Soviet systems, this nation responded by a massive nuclear procurement of its own. The result has been the emergence of weapons systems that will be bad for stability in crisis, bad because they are "designed for prompt and effective attack on each other's weapons and command centers and only indifferently designed for survival in the face of such attack" (pp. 38–41).

is seen to grow out of an already threatening present. What presumably makes the arms race increasingly hazardous is that it promises to lead to ever greater crisis instability. New weapons of greater accuracy and speed will at once sharpen the fear of preemptive attack while encouraging the hope of undertaking such attack successfully should this prove necessary. And ever more complex command and control systems will, beyond a certain level of alert, make increasingly difficult the efforts of political leaders to retain effective control over their nuclear forces.[5]

What is crucial to this view is the contention that *in certain circumstances* the new technologies and the systems for controlling them will prove very dangerous. These circumstances are those of severe crises. In normal circumstances, by contrast, the dangers of the arms race have markedly diminished, when compared to a generation ago. In part this result may be attributed simply to the growing experience of the superpowers in the maintenance of nuclear forces of increasing sophistication. For

---

5. The latter danger is examined at length by Paul Bracken, *The Command and Control of Nuclear Forces* (New Haven: Yale University Press, 1983). Bracken argues that while in normal circumstances the sheer complexity of command and control systems makes them "massively redundant" against the possibility of technical accident, in crisis circumstances the characteristics of the mature system work in the opposite direction. They do so because the nuclear forces of the two superpowers have been horizontally integrated first each with itself and subsequently with the other. This centralization of control, the shift from loose to tight coupling, Bracken states, is "the greatest single shift in nuclear forces during the past twenty years." The result "is a system in which relatively small stimuli in one part produce vast reverberations throughout the rest of the system." What is more, the expansion of sophisticated warning and intelligence systems has also served to link U.S. and Soviet nuclear forces to each other. The result of this linking or tight coupling of the two sides' forces is that a threatening military action by one side can be detected almost immediately by the other side. Although the detected action may not have a clear meaning in the context of an alert, protective measures must be taken against it because of its possible consequences. An action-reaction process is thus begun that has no discernible stopping place short of nuclear war. Bracken concludes that in view of the "ever widening chasm between strategic ideas and the command structure's ability to carry them out," the pervasive uncertainty that has long attended attempts to control nuclear war must now be extended in large measure to nuclear alerts. Indeed, beyond a certain point the decision to go to still higher levels of alert may prove indistinguishable from the decision to go to war.

the most part, though, the diminution of the prospects of accidental war must be attributed to the developments of command and control systems which contain numerous safeguards against the possibility of such war. The likelihood of accidental war is substantially lower today than a generation ago, and may be expected to remain low despite the advent of the new technologies.

So, too, the prospects of a preventive war, of a nuclear strike from out of the blue, are not seen by most expert observers as measurably enhanced. For the residual uncertainties that presently attend and are altogether likely to continue to attend the use of nuclear weapons are such that a coldly planned attack appears almost certain to remain beyond the purview of rational policy choice. To contend otherwise in the case of the Soviet Union requires the assumption that Soviet leadership today is, or tomorrow will be, quite determined to impose its will on us in circumstances that cannot reasonably be interpreted as forcing it to do so and despite having to pay a price that is so high as to be without any real precedent. There is virtually no evidence to support such assumptions.

It is, then, only in periods of severe crisis that the effects of the arms race are properly seen as critical. The case for considering these effects profoundly destabilizing can be summarized thus: when command systems that cannot be reliably controlled are joined to weapons systems that cannot be reliably protected, the stage is set for the breakdown of deterrence. That stage is already partially set by virtue of weapons that can destroy weapons but are themselves vulnerable to attack. It will be completed when the new technologies hold out still greater promise of destroying an adversary's weapons but remain vulnerable to attack. In these circumstances, the speech that the mythical Soviet or American military planner makes to his leaders concludes with these words: "We may suffer a few million casualties, but an adversary will be thoroughly and finally defeated. And if we don't do it to him now, it is he who will be able to win by striking the first blow."[6]

---

6. Gelb, "Is the Nuclear Threat Manageable?" p. 26.

If we but once examine this view with any care, we find that it rests on a truism. For what it says is that when it seems better to strike than to hold back, deterrence will in all likelihood break down. But what are the conditions in which this will be the case? When will it be better to strike than to hold back? Those who draw up scenarios in which deterrence breaks down are saying, in effect, that they will define these conditions. This is not difficult. The critical condition must be the emerging conviction on one or both sides that nuclear war is inevitable but that something—perhaps even a great deal—can be gained by striking first. This conviction is quite compatible with the belief that a preemptive attack will result in far greater costs than gains. For the alternative to attacking may also appear to carry far greater costs than would be the case if one were to strike first rather than second. Another, though less than critical, condition is the existence of weapons that are believed to enhance the promise of preemption, but because of their vulnerability increase the risks of failing to preempt. We may call these weapons destabilizing. And so they are, once a certain stage has been reached in a crisis between nuclear powers. But what has brought the crisis to a point where the "destabilizing" weapons seem almost to "take over" and to undermine deterrence is a political process, a process out of which the conviction increasingly grows that war is inevitable.

Technology does impose dangers of its own and other things being equal, these dangers can be expected to increase if the arms race goes on unchecked. Even so, if there is a necessity at work here, it is not one imposed by technology but by man's nature and the historical situations in which the statesman must act. The limitations technology is seen to place on statecraft must ultimately be found in the limitations of man's nature. The precise relevance of these limitations in a given instance may remain controverted and uncertain. But limitations there are and they will be apparent in weapons systems capable of disarming and destroying an opponent and of doing so within a matter of several minutes. Before these systems can impose a necessity of their own, however, statesmen must have created a situation that enables them to do so. Whatever their characteristics, weapons as such cannot undermine deterrence. To believe otherwise, as many appear to do, is to dissolve politics into technology. What weapons can do is to require a change in the operation of deterrence. They may do so chiefly by changing the point or the threshold beyond which deterrence breaks down and the conviction emerges that war is inevitable.

It is the statesman who undermines deterrence. Moreover, he undermines deterrence not so much by permitting the development of the new technologies as by refusing to recognize that these technologies may require corresponding change in the operation of deterrence. The effects of the arms race on deterrence are commonly misunderstood because the significance of deterrence is, in this respect at least, commonly misunderstood. If deterrence is in substantial part a function of technology, it must change as technology changes. The contention that the kind of crisis we could have a generation ago over missiles in Cuba would prove much more dangerous today does not mean that deterrence has been partially undermined. It does mean that the threshold beyond which deterrence is likely to break down has shifted. One of the tasks of the statesman in the nuclear age, and perhaps his most important task, is to adjust the definition of the nuclear threshold to the conditions that determine it and to bend all efforts to ensure that this threshold is neither crossed nor closely approached.

If these considerations have merit, an apparent obsession over the arms race is for the most part an obsession over the conflict that drives the arms race. An anxiety over technology is in reality largely an anxiety over politics. The great worry over deterrence being undermined by the new weapons is in fact largely a worry over the wisdom, or lack thereof, of political leaders who are today entrusted with the operation of deterrence.

The lapse of faith in deterrence has been laid largely at the doorstep of the Reagan administration. A legion of critics have insisted that this administration must bear a major responsibility for a movement and debate that might have been avoided by a government with a less ideological and less bellicose outlook. One of them has even written that his latecoming to an apocalyptic view of the future is to be attributed to ideologues in Washington who have broken with the outlook of their predecessors. "I no longer have much confidence," Arthur Schlesinger, Jr., writes, "in the admonitory effect of the possession of nuclear weapons."[7] Whereas previous Presidents were sobered by their tragic power to initiate nuclear war, this President is presumably different. He is different because he is in thrall to an ideology that blinds him to the terrible dangers of nuclear war.

The evidence for this blindness consists, in part, of statements made about nuclear weapons and nuclear war by Mr. Reagan as a private citizen or as a candidate for office. Although betraying no particular sophistication about matters nuclear, none of these statements can reasonably be taken as grounds for coming to an apocalyptic view of the future. In the views Mr. Reagan has expressed as President, the case for finding in them a blindness toward the dangers of nuclear war seems even more strained. In the most quoted of these statements, the President responded to a question about whether he believed in the possibility of a limited nuclear war between this country and the Soviet Union in these words: "I could see where you could have the exchange of tactical weapons against troops in the field without it bringing either one of the major powers to pushing the button."[8] Whatever one may think of this response, it scarcely demonstrates the power of ideology in blinding men to the dangers of nuclear war. No doubt, it must arouse those who take as an article of faith that any use of nuclear weapons can lead only to an unlimited nuclear exchange. But there are many people who share Mr. Reagan's skepticism in this matter and who are not, by any reasonable definition, blind ideologues. Whether or

7. Arthur Schlesinger, Jr., "Foreign Policy and the American Character," *Foreign Affairs* (Fall 1983), p. 13.

8. Bernard Gwertzman, "President Says U.S. Should Not Waver in Backing Saudis," *The New York Times*, October 18, 1981, p. 1.

not limited nuclear war in Europe is possible is not a matter to be settled by faith or ideology. Nor did the President in his reply indicate otherwise. If anything, his response was far less dogmatic than the vast majority of utterances on the subject.[9]

The vast majority of utterances, however, are not made by individuals possessed of the power to initiate nuclear war. One lesson to be drawn from the experience of the Reagan administration is simply the rising sensitivity of media and publics to statements about the possible use of nuclear weapons by high public officials, and particularly by the President. This sensitivity has increased with the passage of time to a point where virtually any statement about nuclear weapons or strategy is likely to prove an invitation to trouble. For the public and its elites do not want to be reminded of the basis on which their security ultimately rests. The Reagan administration badly erred initially by not taking this disinclination sufficiently to heart. Instead of glossing over a subject that could be dealt with only at considerable risk, it responded to inquiries that were put to it, and occasionally even offered some gratuitous elaboration. The responses were neither startling for their novelty nor unreasonable in their substance. On balance, they preserved a striking continuity with positions taken by preceding administrations. Still, in the circumstances of the early 1980s, dominated as they have been by growing Soviet-American tension, responses that might otherwise have gone largely unremarked, provoked a series of minor political storms.

The Reagan administration not only tended to talk too much about nuclear matters, but to use an idiom that seemed to confirm the dark suspicions held by many about its intentions. Thus the dismayed and accusatory reaction to the 1982 Defense Guidance statement with its concept of "prevailing" in a protracted nuclear war. American nuclear forces, a critical passage reportedly read, "must prevail and be able to force the Soviet

---

9. One might, for example, compare Mr. Reagan's reply to these remarks of Arthur Schlesinger ("Foreign Policy and the American Character," p. 11): "Little seems to me more dangerous than the current fantasy of controlled and graduated nuclear war. . . . Let us not be bamboozled by models. Once the nuclear threshold is breached, the game is over."

Union to seek earliest possible termination of hostilities on terms favorable to the United States."[10]

The Defense Guidance document did not break new ground. Its essential features added up to little more than a refinement of the Carter administration's 1980 Presidential Directive 59, which in turn built on strategic concepts that may be traced back a generation. From Kennedy to Reagan, no administration has been able to disavow the prospect, however skeptically it may have viewed that prospect, of the controlled use of nuclear weapons. Equally, no administration has been able to disavow the prospect of emerging from a nuclear conflict with some kind of meaningful victory. Unable to disavow these prospects, no administration has been able to disavow the force structure that might make fighting a limited nuclear war possible. It was our least bellicose and most skeptical of recent Presidents who declared during his first year in office that the American strategic arsenal "should be strong enough that a possible nuclear war would end on the most favorable terms possible to the U.S."[11] At the time, 1977, these words of Jimmy Carter did not provoke noticeable criticism. It is true that they do not go quite as far as the 1982 Defense Guidance paper. Still, the difference between ending a nuclear war "on terms favorable to the U.S." rather than "on the most favorable terms possible to the U.S." is scarcely great enough to account for the very different receptions given them.

The Reagan administration has been repeatedly accused of breaking radically from its predecessors in being intent on recapturing the Golden Grail of strategic superiority. This is presumably the meaning of "prevailing," that is, of "concluding hostilities on terms favorable to the U.S.," just as it is the meaning of having a capability that "will insure that the Soviet leadership, by their own calculations, will determine that the price of aggression outweighs any potential benefits." These words of the Reagan-Weinberger Defense Guidance document do indeed

---

10. Cited in Richard Halloran, "Pentagon Draws Up First Strategy For Fighting a Long Nuclear War," *The New York Times*, May 30, 1982, p. 1.

11. Charles Mohr, "Carter Orders Steps to Increase Ability to Meet War Threats," *The New York Times*, August 26, 1977, p. A8.

suggest a kind of strategic superiority. But then, so does the Carter-Brown PD59 "countervailing" strategy. The former Secretary of Defense, Harold Brown, has defined the countervailing strategy in these terms: "to convince the Soviets that they will be successfully opposed at any level of aggression they choose, and that no plausible outcome at any level of conflict could represent 'success' for them by any reasonable definition of success."[12] The countervailing strategy does not posit an American victory. Instead, it promises a Soviet defeat. For it "seeks a situation in which the Soviets would always lose more than they could reasonably expect to gain from either beginning or escalating a military conflict."[13] Is this not, however, a definition of sorts of victory? Unless it is assumed that our losses too are always disproportionate to our gains, in which case there would scarcely be grounds for recommending it, the countervailing strategy does come close to a promise of victory.

The distinction between "countervailing" and "prevailing" is, accordingly, a very thin one. So too, is the difference with respect to the forces required to implement strategy. The charge that is made against the strategy of prevailing, that it implies the effort to regain a position of superiority, might be made with almost equal plausibility against the countervailing strategy. Although the architects of the latter were emphatic in declaring that its implementation required no more than the maintenance of a position of essential equivalence, the declaration suggests otherwise. For it is difficult to see how we might insure that the Soviets will always lose more than they could possibly gain unless we enjoy something that approximates escalation dominance. In turn, escalation dominance implies at least a kind of superiority.

In fact, neither the Carter nor the Reagan administration has pursued a procurement policy designed to achieve strategic superiority. Yet each has articulated a strategic doctrine that implies a kind of superiority. In part, this apparent anomaly is

---

12. Secretary of Defense, *Annual Report to the Congress, FY 1982*, U.S. Department of Defense, January 19, 1981, Washington: GPO, 1981, p. 40.

13. Harold Brown, *Thinking About National Security, Defense and Foreign Policy in a Dangerous World* (Boulder, Colorado: Westview Press, 1983), p. 81.

explained by the need to retain, if only for reasons of morale, some semblance of claim to a theory of victory. Thus Mr. Weinberger's well-known declaration: "You show me a Secretary of Defense who's planning not to prevail and I'll show you a Secretary of Defense who ought to be impeached."[14] In part, however, the explanation must be sought in the American strategic predicament. The root of that predicament is the asymmetrical structure of interest that imposes more difficult and exacting deterrence requirements on the United States than on the Soviet Union. While in the Soviet case these requirements extend no further than to Eastern Europe, in the American case they extend, beyond this hemisphere, to Western Europe, Japan, and the Persian Gulf. To an extent far greater than for the Soviet Union, deterrence for the United States has always been, and remains today, the extension of deterrence to others than the self. By its very nature, extended deterrence must have much less credibility than self-deterrence. This liability of extended deterrence, moreover, cannot be fully compensated for by greater conventional forces. Greater conventional forces will raise the threshold of nuclear conflict but they cannot preclude nuclear conflict. Ultimately, compensation must be found either at the strategic nuclear level or nowhere. But it can only be found at the strategic level by forces that are more than simply the equivalent of the Soviet Union's forces. As we are now painfully aware, equivalence and no more must subject extended deterrence to pervasive and increasingly corrosive doubt.

Since the late 1960s, strategic doctrines have increasingly assumed the function of bridging the growing gap between the forces needed for extended deterrence and the forces in being. If the gap can no longer be bridged in fact, it can still be bridged in word. Without claiming strategic superiority—indeed, even

---

14. Richard Halloran, *The New York Times*, August 12, 1983, p. 8. Characteristically, the Secretary of Defense also declared that although nuclear war was not winnable, "we certainly are planning not to be defeated." In this regard, Michael Howard has noted in discussing Soviet attempts to fit nuclear weapons into a Clausewitzean framework that "one has only to state the opposite of this doctrine to accept that it is in theory unexceptionable, and that it would be difficult for them to say anything else." "On Fighting a Nuclear War," *International Security* (Spring 1981), p. 9.

while disavowing an interest in seeking superiority—the benefits of superiority are nevertheless salvaged in some measure. Thus the claim that we may still ensure that the Soviets would always lose more than they could expect to gain from resorting to any kind of armed aggression. Or the claim that in a nuclear conflict our forces will have the capability of imposing an early termination of the conflict on terms favorable to this country.

In proclaiming the strategy of prevailing, the Reagan administration simply followed an established practice, though perhaps it did so too exuberantly. What is important is that it did so at a time when détente had clearly broken down and tension between the superpowers was rising to a level that had not been experienced since the years of the classic cold war. In these circumstances, the doctrine of prevailing was subject to a scrutiny it might not and probably would not have otherwise received. In these same circumstances, the earlier doctrine of countervailing power was subject to a criticism considerably harsher than the criticism that marked its appearance in 1980.

The real indictment made of the initial years of the Reagan administration was not of its military strategy but of its politics. It was not so much what Mr. Reagan said about nuclear weapons and their possible use that aroused opponents, but what he said about the Soviet Union. In word and in spirit, though not in action, this administration largely returned to the period of the classic cold war. It did so, however, in strategic circumstances which were bleak by comparison with the circumstances that characterized this earlier period.

The classic cold war began with an American monopoly of nuclear weapons. It ended, if we take the period immediately following the Cuban missile crisis as marking its end, with this country still enjoying a position of strategic superiority over the Soviet Union. A nuclear revisionism now contends that, contrary to what has been the conventional wisdom, strategic superiority is useless, in that it cannot be translated into diplomatic power or political advantage, and that this inutility was dramatically demonstrated at the time of the Cuban missile crisis. In turn, this view of strategic superiority is part of a larger assessment of the significance of nuclear weapons, an assessment in which the utility of these weapons is found to be very limited. Few have been prepared to go quite as far as George Kennan in declaring that "the nuclear bomb is the most useless weapon ever invented. . . . It is not even an effective defense against itself."[15] Instead, the more moderate revisionist view is expressed by a former Secretary of Defense: "Nuclear weapons serve no military purpose whatsoever. They are totally useless—except only to deter one's opponent from using them."[16]

If nuclear weapons are useful only for deterring the use of nuclear weapons, if strategic superiority cannot be employed to any meaningful advantage, then clearly a good deal of the conventional wisdom respecting the history of the postwar period must be discounted. Neither the American monopoly of nuclear weapons at the start of this period nor the subsequent American strategic superiority conferred any advantage on us. Indeed, if the revisionist view is to be literally credited, the existence of nuclear weapons and the fear of nuclear war had little to do with the maintenance of peace in Europe. If nuclear weapons deter only the use of nuclear weapons, they do not and cannot account for the absence of wars fought with conventional arms.

The consequences of nuclear revisionism, if once pursued to their logical conclusion, are quite startling. This does not mean that they are wrong. It does mean that we are well advised

---

15. George Kennan, *The Nuclear Delusion* (New York: Pantheon Books, 1983), p. 175. Given Kennan's view of the unusability of nuclear weapons, it is quite understandable that he thinks these weapons can threaten or intimidate only people who wish to be intimidated. Thus the West Europeans need not feel intimidated by Soviet missiles unless they wish to be. See Kennan, "Zero Options," *The New York Review of Books* (May 12, 1983), p. 17.

16. Robert McNamara, "The Military Role of Nuclear Weapons," *Foreign Affairs* (Fall 1983), p. 79. This exception alone is not insubstantial. When taken together with the inhibitory effect nuclear weapons have on the employment of conventional weapons by one nuclear power against another, an effect that the nuclear revisionists do not contest, the "inutility" theme begins to look more modest. This is so even if we discount altogether the intimidating effects of nuclear weapons.

to be skeptical of these efforts to recast our understanding of the history of the recent past, particularly when it is apparent that these efforts are motivated by and put in the service of the disputes of the present. Now that many have concluded that, in present circumstances, nuclear weapons are "useless," they apparently must persuade themselves, and others, that this has always been the case. But even if this were the case today, it was not the case in the past. Strategic superiority did confer advantages so long as we clearly enjoyed it. It did make extended deterrence quite credible—and if not *quite* credible than at least *more* credible—and it is on the credibility of extended deterrence that the structure of American interests and commitments ultimately rested yesterday and, in far more difficult circumstances, continues to rest today.

The strategic superiority we once enjoyed also made it much easier for us to sustain a faith in deterrence. That faith was not shaken by the Cuban missile crisis. However chastening the crisis was for the immediate participants, in terms of demonstrating more vividly than ever before the dangers held out by the conflict with the Soviet Union, the public generally viewed its outcome as a victory brought about by our commanding advantage in both conventional and strategic nuclear forces. The crisis brought to light the marked disparity between our intercontinental missile force and that of the Soviet Union. The significance of this disparity has since been virtually dismissed by a number of those who at the time held high office and were members of the Executive Committee constituted to advise the President on the crisis.[17] They have pointed out that the possibility of using nuclear weapons was never considered.[18] Moreover,

---

17. McGeorge Bundy has recently reminded us that: "Along with five other members of the Kennedy Administration, including Dean Rusk and Robert McNamara, I have written that the missile crisis illustrates 'not the significance but the insignificance of nuclear superiority in the face of survivable thermonuclear retaliatory forces'." ("Atomic Diplomacy Reconsidered," p. 35.)

18. George Ball, a member of the Committee, has noted that while the Committee did not believe that the actions they were considering would trigger a Soviet nuclear response, "We could not . . . free our minds of the awful possibility that if we made even the slightest mistake, we might start our country up an escalator that could lead to a nuclear exchange." "The Cosmic Bluff," *The*

they have noted that the disparity between the two sides' forces still could not have prevented the Soviet Union from imposing unprecedented destruction on this country.[19] But these considerations do not disprove that the strategic superiority we enjoyed at the time of the crisis had no effect on Soviet leadership. They show, instead, that it did not have an effect on American leadership in the sense that it did not prompt the Kennedy administration to attempt directly to exploit this superiority. To the contrary, President Kennedy and his associates explicitly refused to do so. At the same time, there was no disposition to refuse the indirect exploitation of strategic superiority. Such exploitation followed simply from the existence of a crisis in which the distinct possibility arose of the superpowers becoming directly engaged in a conventional military conflict.

In the decade or so following the Cuban missile crisis, the loss of strategic superiority had no more than a marginal impact on this nation's faith in deterrence. Although the Soviet achievement of strategic parity was an event of first-order importance, requiring a rethinking of the entire American security position, its effects on the structure of extended deterrence attracted only moderate attention and caused even less anxiety. In contrast to the early 1960s, the early 1970s gave rise to almost no agitation in the body politic over the nuclear issue, despite the momentous changes that had occurred.

New York Review of Books (July 21, 1982), pp. 37–8. It hardly seems unreasonable to assume that if this possibility weighed so heavily on the American side, it weighed even more on the Soviet side, given the latter's inferiority in strategic nuclear forces.

19. This is of course the most common claim. It is emphasized by Fred Kaplan in his interesting and instructive account of the Cuban missile crisis, *The Wizards of Armageddon* (New York: Simon & Schuster, 1983), pp. 210–50. The point that emerges from this and other accounts is simply that by any reasonable calculation made at the time of American casualties in a nuclear exchange, the consequences were such as to appall the President and his chief advisors. Yet the fact remains that these projected consequences did not deter the Kennedy administration from pursuing a course that might well have eventuated in a conventional clash of arms, a clash that would have raised a substantial possibility of nuclear conflict. In such conflict we would very likely have suffered unprecedented casualties, but the Soviet Union would have been destroyed.

Vietnam apart, the reason for this extraordinary unconcern was that we were in the floodtide of détente. Having developed slowly and unevenly in the course of the 1960s, by the early 1970s détente had become the centerpiece of the Nixon policy reformulation. In the context of détente, the loss of strategic superiority was generally seen as an event without great significance. Instead, far more attention was directed to the Strategic Arms Limitation Talks (SALT), though in retrospect the results of these negotiations, embodied in the 1972 Moscow accords, appear almost inconsequential in comparison with the Soviet Union's achievement of strategic parity. But the arms control negotiations were considered almost from the outset a litmus test of the overall relationship of the superpowers. If this relationship was relatively good, the possible consequences of the Soviet Union having achieved strategic parity might be taken in stride. Besides, the Soviet achievement did not challenge the regnant view that the preservation of mutual deterrence was best guaranteed by both sides maintaining a retaliatory force with the capability of assured destruction. The Moscow agreements were successfully defended as preserving mutual deterrence while stabilizing it by limiting the buildup of nuclear forces.

It was in this manner that public faith in deterrence was sustained during the 1970s, despite the continuing buildup of Soviet strategic forces. Although by the middle of the decade, the structure of détente had begun to give way, it did not visibly disintegrate until 1980. While it lasted, faith in deterrence went largely unquestioned. It is in the fall of détente and the rise of a new cold war that we must find the simple but critical explanation for the prominence now given to nuclear weapons and the prospect of nuclear war.

The Reagan administration could have moderated public reaction to the nuclear arms issue had it shown from the outset greater receptivity to arms control and had it generally observed greater discretion in its statements on nuclear issues. It could not have escaped a substantial reaction, though, even had it acted with far greater circumspection than it did. Indeed, after a first term in office, and many mistakes, the administration has learned a great deal about guarding its tongue, making pious gestures, and even playing the role of true believer in arms control. Still, the anti-nuclear arms movement and the nuclear debate persist. They persist because they are a response essentially to the breakdown of détente and to the dangers of war this breakdown is thought to raise.

The striking continuity in the nuclear debate of the 1980s with the debate of a generation earlier has already been noted. So too, the essentially unchanging dimensions of the nuclear dilemma have been given as the explanation of this continuity. Are there any recent developments, however, that might have the effect of fundamentally altering the now familiar dimensions of the nuclear dilemma? Of course, one such development, the Reagan administration's strategic defense initiative, holds out the ultimate prospect of transcending the dilemma altogether. Nuclear weapons would be rendered obsolete by virtue of defensive systems that destroyed these weapons with virtually perfect effectiveness. The age of deterrence would thus be left behind. But we are here considering developments that—though they do not take us beyond the age of deterrence—nevertheless change significantly the terms of the nuclear dilemma. Since the heart of that dilemma is one of limits, a basic change might be effected by the conclusive demonstration either of no limits at all to the destructiveness of nuclear war or, conversely, of quite clear limits. In the one case the threat would arise of a nation's, if not humanity's, utter extinction. A global climatic catastrophe resulting from nuclear war has been offered in evidence of this position. In another case, the promise would beckon of a return to a form of warfare that could effectively distinguish between combatants and noncombatants. New weapons which are revolutionary in their accuracy have been offered in evidence of the latter position.

The prospect of a global climatic catastrophe consequent upon a nuclear war recalls to mind Herman Kahn's Doomsday Machine. The Doomsday Machine was programmed to set off the Doomsday Bombs, thereby destroying civilization, should the Soviet Union commit an act of nuclear aggression that went above a certain threshold. Once set up, it was to be independent of human control. The Soviet Union was to be duly informed of its existence. The purpose of the machine was to perfect deterrence.

"Nuclear winter," as it is described, may be regarded as nature's equivalent of the Doomsday Machine. A nuclear war that goes beyond a certain threshold would result in a climatic catastrophe.[20] The prospect of nuclear winter would at last compel men to do what their political and moral inventiveness have never been able to do. Once war holds out the certainty of mutual—indeed, of universal—destruction, it will be abandoned. Nuclear winter appears as the final confirmation of the very old idea that the institution of war contains within itself the means for achieving its own disappearance. All it need do is become sufficiently destructive.

Many believe that if the nuclear winter findings are scientifically sound, the political and strategic consequences are potentially very great. It is quite true that below the threshold of climatic disaster nuclear wars could still be fought. The worry has been expressed that without any further advances in arms control, the United States and the Soviet Union might simply "develop smaller but more accurate strategic nuclear warheads, for use at levels below the threshold of the nuclear winter" and that in the longer term "there may still be a risk of preemption and hence a more precarious balance of terror."[21] But if the nuclear threshold is quite modest, the fear of exceeding it would be likely to prove quite constraining. How constraining beyond the constraints already operative must remain conjectural. For those who have the capability to set off a nuclear winter also have the capability to destroy one another directly by the employment of nuclear force. That such direct destruction would not lead to global catastrophe as well, can scarcely be of any comfort to

20. For a review of these findings and possible policy implications, see Carl Sagan, "Nuclear War and Climatic Catastrophe," *Foreign Affairs* (Winter 1983/84), pp. 257–92.

21. Dan Horowitz and Robert J. Lieber, "Nuclear Winter," Comment and Correspondence, *Foreign Affairs* (Spring 1984), p. 996.

them. Even so, the prospect of nuclear winter clearly must reinforce inhibitions already at work.

Is the nuclear winter analysis valid? Indeed, is there any reliable way by which the hypothesis of a climatic catastrophe might be tested other than by a way that risks the catastrophic event itself? If not, will not the nuclear winter danger become yet another of the great unknowns surrounding nuclear weapons? And as such, will it not fall victim to the politicization that seems to claim almost any issue bearing on nuclear weapons?

Anxiety over the apocalyptic effects of setting off nuclear explosions have been given scientific expression before, only to be subsequently considered unfounded or grossly exaggerated. The same could happen in the case of the analysis given of the climatic effects of nuclear weapons. Scientific opinion remains divided on the implications of using nuclear weapons in the atmosphere, and it would not be surprising if this division were to persist. Even so, what is sobering about the nuclear winter analysis is that after almost four decades we have only now come to an awareness—and then quite by accident—of a potentially grave danger attendant upon the use of nuclear weapons. The thought obviously occurs: what other dangers might there be? Nuclear winter is an indication of how little we may yet know about the consequences of nuclear war. It points to the limited control, if control at all, we may have over those consequences.

The development of ever more accurate weapons appears to point in quite the opposite direction. The prospect of weapons that when once perfected will permit force to be employed with great accuracy at great distances, Albert Wohlstetter has written, is "in some ways more revolutionary than the transition from conventional to fission explosives or even fusion weapons." The reason is that an improvement in accuracy "by a factor of 100 improves blast effectiveness against a small, hard military target about as much as multiplying the energy released a million times." Once we can, in Wohlstetter's words, hit what we aim at and only what we aim at, we can also closely limit collateral damage. "It is the lack of technology smart enough, rather than the availability of large brute-force single weapons, that lies at the root of the problem of collateral damage."[22]

The new technology of smart weapons is thus found to alter fundamentally both the strategic and moral dilemmas nuclear weapons have heretofore posed. It is not the first time that this claim has been put forward. In the 1950s, a similar claim was made on behalf of tactical nuclear weapons. In the 1960s, the same contention was made in support of flexible response and counterforce. Each was a response to the same fundamental problem: the existence of the potential for unlimited destruction, along with the continued possibility of war. Each was a manifestation of the impulse to provide for intermediate stages of violence, to create rungs on the escalation ladder short of catastrophic destruction. In each case, the effort has been to discriminate, whether according to the type of weapon used, the targets, or the theatre of war. And for each new intermediate stage, or form of discrimination, the relevant questions have always been the same. Is discrimination possible? If possible, will it prove provocative? If war does begin, regardless of the technical possibilities for discrimination, will it remain limited?

These questions, not surprisingly, are being raised again with respect to the smart weapons. Even if the discrimination and control claimed on their behalf are born out—something that itself will not be easy to determine short of war—will not the new weapons encourage the belief that war—excluding general war—has again become a manageable enterprise? In turn, will not the growth of that belief create a greater likelihood of war? If the persuasion once takes root that the problem of collateral damage has now been resolved and that nuclear weapons have now been domesticated, will not the effect be to undermine the great barrier against general war that has grown up in the nuclear age?

Provided they live up to advance expectations, the new

22. Albert Wohlstetter, "Bishops, Statesmen, and other Strategists on the Bombing of Innocents," *Commentary* (June 1983), pp. 15–35. In a similar vein, Robert Jastrow, "Reagan or the Scientists: Why the President Is Right about Missile Defense," *Commentary* (January 1984), pp. 23–32.

weapons will indeed give us choices that we did not have before. They will extend the spectrum of violence. They will add a number of intermediate levels, between the upper and lower extremes of this spectrum. But they will not solve the great political and moral dilemma created by nuclear weapons of finding reasonably clear and effective limits to force. The distinctive danger presented by nuclear weapons will persist, though now it may well be mitigated by the existence of weapons that afford a markedly greater opportunity to act in a restrained and discriminate manner.

The view that finds a salvation of sorts in the new weapons assumes that men have been indiscriminate in the conduct of war because they lacked the means to be discriminate—or, at any rate, more discriminate. This is a partial truth that, in the manner of all partial truths, becomes dangerous when taken as the whole truth. Indiscriminate or immoderate means decree immoderate ends. Yet discriminate or moderate means may also be used in the pursuit of immoderate ends. Men have been indiscriminate in the conduct of war, in part, because they have sought indiscriminate or unlimited ends. Should they continue to seek those ends, the threat of indiscriminate warfare must persist, smart weapons notwithstanding.

It will not do, then, to assume that the advent of smart weapons will permit us to combine discriminating means with any of a wide variety of ends. That side against which the most accurate weapons are used in pursuit of immoderate ends may still be driven to threaten and to employ indiscriminate weapons. The new technology does not resolve the issue of limits. Nor could it be expected to do so.

The element of continuity in the present debate can be overdone. If from one perspective today's debate looks like nothing so much as a rerun of yesterday, from yet another perspective it appears quite different. Although the framework and essential terms of the present debate are the same as those of the past, its tenor has changed. In the course of a generation, there has been a considerable shift of position with respect to the legitimacy of nuclear weapons.

The significance of this shift cannot be found in the questions that are asked today; they are similar to those of a generation ago. Instead, it is in the choice of answers increasingly given to familiar questions. Thus, when the American Catholic bishops declare that "nuclear weapons particularly and nuclear warfare as it is planned today raise new moral questions," the referent point can only be the world of pre-nuclear weapons. The fashionably banal phrase that the world is now "wired for destruction" might just as truthfully have been uttered in the 1960s. It is not the essential predicament nuclear weapons have created for us that is novel today but the evaluation increasingly made of that predicament. The bishops are much closer to the mark in observing that "what previously had been defined as a safe and stable system of deterrence is today viewed with political and moral skepticism." A predicament, they justly observe, that once had been widely accepted with little question, "is now being subjected to the sharpest criticism" and "evaluated with a new perspective."

The bishops' letter is a significant part of this new perspective. A generation ago, in 1965, the second Vatican Council expressed a quite different perspective.[23] What the Vatican Council condemned was "total war" and any acts of war "aimed indiscriminately at the destruction of entire cities or extensive areas along with their population." What the American Catholic bishops condemn is virtually any and every possible form of nuclear war. The use of nuclear weapons is rejected, whether these weapons are used against military targets or against civilian centers of population, whether in a first strike or a retaliatory second strike, whether in a strategic or theatre nuclear war. The rejection is almost complete. Nor does it matter that the bishops' position is based on the conviction that the use of nuclear weapons cannot be controlled and that the effects cannot be

---

23. Cf. Second Vatican Council, *Pastoral Constitution on the Church in the Modern World, December 7, 1965* (National Catholic Welfare Conference, 1966). The statement on war appears in Part II, Chap. 5.

limited, considerations that are not, after all, very different from those emphasized by Vatican Council II. What does matter is that the bishops invoke these considerations to condemn nuclear war almost without qualification, while Vatican II invoked them to form only a carefully qualified statement about the circumstances in which the use of nuclear weapons would be illegitimate.

The position taken by the Catholic bishops toward nuclear war is quite close to the position of many who make up the deterrence faithful. "Of course," Leon Wieseltier writes, "there can be no nuclear war that is just. There is no moral standard that can sanction it."[24] There can never be a just nuclear war, if it is assumed that no meaningful limits can or will be set to the conduct of such war. Given that assumption, nuclear war must either destroy the ends for which it is presumably fought or result in destruction that is disproportionate to those ends and that is, in any event, indiscriminate. In either case—or, what is generally held more likely, in both cases—nuclear war must prove unjust.

This condemnation of nuclear war—any and every nuclear war—cannot but have a bearing on the moral assessment of deterrence. If the use of nuclear weapons must prove immoral because they cannot be controlled or their effects limited, deterrence structures that rest on the threat to use these weapons are also likely to be seen as illegitimate. What gives these structures their one and only saving grace is the promise that they will never have to be put to active use. Even then, the justification of deterrence will largely rest on the grounds of necessity. Yet the plea of necessity, taken alone, can never prove quite satisfactory. If deterrent structures are to be given the requisite support for sustained periods, they must be seen as responding to something more than necessity. That plea might alone suffice if these structures were securely endowed with the quality of certainty. Since they cannot be so endowed, the slightest lapse of faith in the reliability of deterrence must give rise to a growing sense of despair—moral and otherwise.

The bishops' letter clearly points in this direction and, ac-

---

24. Wieseltier, *Nuclear War, Nuclear Peace*, p. 28.

cordingly, has the effect of weakening deterrence. It does so not only by coming very close to a position of "no use—ever" but by undermining the legitimacy of deterrence even while giving deterrence a "strictly conditioned moral acceptance." Yet it is not only bishops' letters and the like that undermine deterrence. In a way that is less apparent, though perhaps no less effective, so do the champions of minimum deterrence. For their position, too, comes very close to one of "no use—ever"—certainly it does so in spirit. What else can be the meaning of their counsel that in the event deterrence fails, the overriding duty of the statesman is to try to bring the war to an end as quickly as possible and without regard to other considerations? If this is the great goal of the statesman, to which all else must be subordinated, the question arises: why should the side made the object of a preemptive strike—presumably this country—respond at all? To do nothing in response to a nuclear attack would likely hold out the best prospect of bringing the conflict to an end in the quickest and least destructive way.

The combination of renouncing a preemptive attack and of commiting oneself to terminating a nuclear war "as quickly as possible and with the least amount of damage possible—on both sides"[25] is surely clearly something very close to the bishops' "no use—ever." The threat of a second strike may serve a deterrent purpose. But even that purpose may be substantially negated by the commitment, if it is generally known, to war termination as quickly as possible. Indeed, as between the bishops' commitment to "no use—ever" and a minimum deterrence with the above commitment, the difference appears negligible. Of course, a position of minimum deterrence need not bear this commitment. But if it should not, what then would be the purpose served by the second strike? The question was raised a generation ago. It has yet to be answered satisfactorily.

---

25. This is Bernard Brodie's dictum, cited above. In a recent essay, Theodore Draper quotes Brodie approvingly, while admitting that he "does not pretend to know how it will be possible to terminate a nuclear war with the least possible damage. . . . This very uncertainty is an element of deterrence." "Nuclear Temptations," *The New York Review of Books* (January 19, 1984), p. 49. This must rank as a classic case in which ignorance is bliss.

Given the assumptions of minimum deterrence, a second strike must in all likelihood prove strategically pointless and morally perverse.

Is it unfair to conclude, then, that the bishops' position is the moral analogue of the strategic position of minimum deterrence? What to the former is morally proscribed, to the latter is strategically absurd. To both, deterrence is justified only if it need never be "acted out." Given this similarity, it is less important that what the bishops may not "intend" doing, the supporters of minimum deterrence may intend to their hearts' content. Far more important is the widespread agreement on the immorality of any and all nuclear war.

How may we account for the change that has occurred with respect to the legitimacy of nuclear weapons? A number of observers have taken note of the change, though few have inquired into its possible causes. In part, this absence of speculation is no doubt due to the persuasion that the principal reasons for the shift are self-evident. The public has simply awakened at last to the dangers held out by nuclear weapons; it has become aware of the nature of the catastrophe that would ensue if these weapons were ever to be used. In this view, all that needs explaining is why the public took so long to awaken to the dangers. But once it had done so, it was only to be expected that the condemnation of nuclear weapons would follow. Thus George Ball, writing of the "long overdue" awakening of public interest in, and concern for the military use of, the atom, takes it as self-evident that this interest must lead, as in Ball's judgement it already has led, to enveloping nuclear weapons in a "rigid taboo."[26] To understand these weapons—to know that they cannot be controlled in use and effect and therefore cannot in fact

---

26. George Ball, "The Cosmic Bluff," p. 37. And George Kennan is of the view that at the heart of the anti-nuclear movement is "a growing appreciation by many people of the true horrors of nuclear war." *The Nuclear Delusion*, p. 193.

be employed to achieve a political objective—is to condemn them. The sense that nuclear weapons are illegitimate is synonymous with a growing awareness of them.

It is an appealing view if only because of the role and motive it imputes to the great public. Until quite recently, we are asked to believe, the public regarded the esoteric realm of nuclear weapons and strategy with a detachment bordering on indifference. It did so presumably because it was kept, and was content to be kept, at a discreet distance from matters nuclear and because it largely dismissed the prospect of nuclear war. "So long as Americans regarded the danger of nuclear war as remote and unreal," George Ball notes, "most were content to leave nuclear weapons to academic experts, military theorists, and science fiction writers." But once the Soviet-American relationship began to deteriorate badly at the end of the 1970s, the veil was suddenly torn from before the public's eyes. The danger of nuclear war was no longer seen as remote and unreal. The sudden appreciation of the danger led to the anti-nuclear weapons movement and, synonymous with the movement, to the growing sense that nuclear weapons are illegitimate.

Although appealing, it is an implausible account. It is implausible if only because it distorts the history of the past few decades. The development of nuclear weapons and strategy is seen as taking place almost on a different planet as far as the public is concerned. One would never know from this account that America's nuclear monopoly in the late 1940s was widely credited, whether rightly or wrongly, with deterring a Soviet attack on Western Europe; that a strategy of massive retaliation formed a mainstay of American policy in the 1950s; that the great crisis of the early 1960s over Cuba was provoked by placing nuclear missiles on the island and was resolved only at the risk of a war between the superpowers that might have led in turn to the use of nuclear weapons; and that a decade of much publicized arms control negotiations had occurred during the 1970s, which at the least maintained public awareness of the nuclear weapons issue, and at the most, by constant repetition of the need to control the dangers of the arms race, prepared the ground for the movement that sprang up once these negotiations—and the superpower relationship so closely identified with them—began to collapse.

Given these and yet other developments, it is scarcely credible to picture the past several years as the period of a great awakening of the public to the physical and moral perils of nuclear weapons. Neither an older nor, for that matter, a younger generation was oblivious to the perils of nuclear war. The destructiveness of nuclear weapons has long been an integral part of the informal educational curriculum of this society. To argue that it is only recently that the public has come to appreciate what the arms race means or what nuclear war means is either to claim far too much for public understanding or far too little. The public cannot be expected to know what the experts continue to disagree over. But the public can be expected to know and does know the general considerations that condition the persisting controversy over nuclear weapons.

The change in attitude toward nuclear weapons that has undoubtedly occurred in the past generation is not so much the result of a heightened understanding of the characteristics of these weapons and the dangers of nuclear war as it is of a heightened appreciation of the increasing power at the disposal of the Soviet Union. There are, of course, other reasons for this change. Nuclear weapons are increasingly seen as illegitimate, in part because force in general is increasingly seen as illegitimate. A changed attitude toward the use of armed force generally explains the changed attitude toward the use of nuclear force. In turn, a changed attitude toward armed force must be attributed in part to the continuing impact of Vietnam. In part it also reflects deeper changes occurring in American society that militate against this most ancient activity of collectives. In time, the deeper explanation of the reaction to Vietnam may well be found in the transformation of American society in directions prophesied long ago by some of the great nineteenth-century sociologists. Derided earlier in this century, the view that liberal-capitalist societies are inherently pacific—and even pacifist—is one that can no longer be readily dismissed.

These considerations are necessarily speculative, but the significance of the increased power of the Soviet Union in effecting a changed attitude toward nuclear weapons in this country seems much less so. The visible ability of the Soviet Union effectively to match any threat of nuclear force on our part clearly has played a considerable role in prompting the reevaluation, moral and otherwise, of nuclear weapons. It is not the first time that the fear of retaliation in kind has led to a display of heightened moral sensitivity. Moralists are understandably reluctant to acknowledge the effect that considerations of reciprocity have in these matters. Their reluctance does not diminish the significance of reciprocity in placing restraints on behavior, and particularly collective behavior.

Unless we are to assume a moral transformation of sorts, never a very promising assumption, an altered view of the legitimacy of nuclear weapons reflects an altered distribution of this form of power. The marked growth of Soviet strategic power in the past generation has been reflected in other ways as well. In the absence of this consideration it would be very difficult to account for the hardening of the conviction that nuclear weapons, any and all nuclear weapons, must prove indiscriminate in their effects, when in practice weapons developments for the first time hold out the solid promise of introducing an appreciable element of discrimination. From a broader perspective, the growth of Soviet military power is reflected in the widespread disposition to minimize, if not almost dismiss, the importance of other differences in accounting for the persistence of the conflict between the Soviet Union and this country. A generation ago, differences in ideology, values, and political structures were still accorded a prime importance. Today, their role in explaining the persistence of the conflict is much reduced. Yet an image of the Soviet Union that has changed substantially for the better since the mid-1960s contrasts strikingly with the reality of the Soviet government's conduct at home and abroad—a reality that scarcely bears out this optimistic image.

Undoubtedly, a more benign image of the Soviet Union is in part the result of the disappearance of the worst features of Stalinism. In part, it is also a consequence of the sheer imcompetence that marks so much of the behavior of the Soviet regime at home and abroad. The repeated demonstration of this incompetence in recent years contrasts vividly with the awe that Stalin was able to create in the West. In part, however, a less threatening image is also the response to the Soviet Union's growth in military power. Given the destruction this power could inflict on the United States, and the world, there is an eminently understandable will to believe that those controlling such power are not only responsible but have no profound conflicts with us. Unhappily, serious conflicts of interest do persist, though their persistence provides no justification for threatening the kinds of measures the two great adversaries continue to threaten.

Whatever the precise explanation of the change in attitude toward nuclear weapons, it seems very likely that the change will persist. For the circumstances that must roughly account for it are not of a transient character. The unrest and disaffection that are the result of this change can only be kept at tolerable levels by a restoration of faith in deterrence. Whether and how such restoration may be effected, or, for that matter, should be effected are the questions around which the nuclear debate has increasingly centered.

DETERRENCE AND THE RESTORATION OF FAITH
The Nuclear Debate II

Is it possible to restore a former faith in deterrence? And even if possible, is it desirable to do so? In the persisting debate over nuclear weapons and strategy, the former question remains critical. Yet it is the latter question that has suddenly and unexpectedly come to the fore. It has done so because for the first time since the age of deterrence began, an administration has betrayed serious skepticism about deterrence. At the close of its first term in office, the Reagan administration broke with what in the course of a generation had become a pattern of behavior for administrations. It did so by beginning to voice its apparently deep-rooted doubts about the possibility and even the desirability of restoring a former faith in deterrence.

The result was to transform virtually overnight the nuclear debate. The years 1981 to 1984 had been dominated by the antinuclear weapons movement, a movement whose principal motivation appeared to be a sudden lapse of faith in deterrence and whose principal demand was to freeze the deployment, testing, and manufacture of all nuclear weapons by the superpowers. The Reagan administration responded to this demand of the peace movement with a firm rejection.

During these same years, the attendant debate over nuclear

strategy, while also stimulated in large part by the breakdown of détente and a renewed fear of war with the Soviet Union, traced the now familiar fault line separating those who believe that deterrence follows largely from the very existence of nuclear weapons from those who believe that a credible theory of use must be developed if deterrence is to be assured. This debate, which reflected even as it obscured marked and often profound differences over Soviet motivation and behavior, was almost as old as nuclear weapons. In the early 1980s, it remained as deep and uncertain as ever.

The Reagan administration not only set its face against the peace movement, in the renewed debate over nuclear strategy it plainly opposed anything even faintly resembling views of "existential" deterrence. It had, after all, come to office after a campaign in which it had emphasized the great danger created by the growth of Soviet land missiles. These missiles, it was argued, had opened, or would soon do so, a "window of vulnerability" for America. The new administration dedicated its efforts to closing that window. It went further and proclaimed a strategy of "prevailing" that implied the attempt to recapture a kind of superiority. And the remarks by its highest officials that were so effectively exploited by critics were invariably remarks that reflected the need to develop a credible theory of use, however limited and modest, if deterrence was to be assured.

This was, in brief, the state of affairs during years that now appear as the first phase of a debate that promises to go on indefinitely. In the succeeding phase of this debate, which began in late 1984, the terms have been set almost entirely by the administration and largely in response to a need to articulate an arms control position. To be sure, this need was itself a response to public pressures, and not only the pressures represented by the peace movement. Yet in responding to those pressures, the administration betrayed an attitude toward the structure of deterrence we have lived with for a generation that was not unlike the attitude of those whose anxiety over the prospects of nuclear war it had earlier dismissed.

The peace movement had been marked above all by a sudden lapse of faith in deterrence. The administration had altered its initial position on the utility of arms control in response to the pressures of the peace movement. Yet its response to those pressures was dominated by the vision of the President's Strategic Defense Initiative (SDI), an initiative that in its own way reflected the same lack of faith in deterrence as did the peace movement. Introduced to the public in a presidential address of March 23, 1983, the initiative, after a brief flurry of public interest and debate, appeared almost to gather dust. The appearance was deceptive. Fervently supported by the President, the initiative suddenly became the vital center of the American position on nuclear strategy and arms control. It informed the new "strategic concept" that was articulated at the beginning of 1985 and that announced this government's intention to lead the world from the present system of mutual deterrence, through a period of transition, to effective non-nuclear defensive forces against offensive nuclear arms, and ultimately to the elimination of all nuclear arms.[1]

The administration's strategic concept was not novel as an idea. Speculation on the prospects of eventually redressing offensive nuclear arms by means of defensive arms had been a recurring feature of the nuclear age. It had been dismissed as a technological fantasy. Recently, a scheme for the abolition of nuclear weapons had been proposed by Jonathan Schell, one of the more prominent writers in the peace movement.[2] Schell's scheme, however, depended on politics rather than on technology and for this reason lacked any attraction for those who have always looked to technology for eventual salvation from the

---

1. The President's speech on defense spending and defensive technology may be found in "Weekly Compilation of Presidential Documents," March 28, 1983, vol. 19, no. 12. The text of the new "strategic concept" reads: "For the next 10 years, we should seek a radical reduction in the number and power of existing and planned offensive and defensive nuclear arms, whether land based or otherwise. We should even now be looking forward to a period of transition, beginning possibly 10 years from now, to effective non-nuclear defensive forces, including defenses against offensive nuclear arms. This period of transition should lead to the eventual elimination of nuclear arms, both offensive and defensive. A nuclear free world is an ultimate objective to which we, and the Soviet Union and all other nations can agree." *The New York Times*, January 26, 1985, pp. 1, 4.

2. See Jonathan Schell, *The Abolition* (1984).

nuclear peril. Even so, what was significant about the proposal advanced by Schell was the growing conviction it reflected about mutual deterrence.

Now another scheme for the abolition of nuclear weapons was proposed, and not only by a President, but by this President. Not unexpectedly, the President's strategic vision provoked comparisons from more than one observer.[3] For both Jonathan Schell and Ronald Reagan, it was noted, the goal we must now strive after is the transcendence of mutual deterrence and not its mere enhancement. But what was often overlooked is that the transcendence of deterrence must become the great and urgent objective of policy only if those responsible for making it so believe that the present structure of deterrence is deeply flawed.

It is quite true that President Reagan has never justified his defense initiative explicitly in these terms. Instead, he has emphasized the desirability of escaping from a world in which it is "necessary to rely on the specter of retaliation, on mutual threat."[4] This arrangement, he has declared on a number of occasions, is a "sad commentary on the human race." It is, of course, just that. But the critical issue here is not whether the deterrent arrangements under which we now live are sad, and morally oppressive, but whether they are dangerous. Clearly it would be preferable not to have to rely on the specter of retaliation. Clearly it would be better, in the President's words, "to save lives rather than to avenge them." Experience has shown, however, that such reliance is quite tolerable so long as there is sufficient belief in its effectiveness. It is the displacement of belief by skepticism in high places that must now give pause over the future of deterrence. What began yesterday as a lapse of faith on the part of a protest movement, has today spread to encompass an administration. High officials who only yesterday dismissed proposals for a nuclear freeze as radical and utopian,

---

3. The most perceptive was Leon Wieseltier, "Nuclear Idealism, Nuclear Realism," *The New Republic* (March 11, 1985), pp. 20–25. The President, Wieseltier argues, has joined the peace movement "in the delegitimation of deterrence."

4. This and the immediately following quotes are taken from President Reagan's address of March 23, 1983.

today profess to find realism in a policy that points to the goal of a world that is rid altogether of nuclear weapons.

The Reagan administration's apparent lapse of faith in deterrence should not have come as a surprise. That lapse was foreshadowed not only by the President's March 1983 speech. It was also foreshadowed by the long growing dissatisfaction by numerous conservatives with what they had always seen as an arrangement that, at best, was no more than tolerable. In one important respect, at least, their attitude was shared by many others, though in lesser degree. Mutual deterrence, the condition in which we have now lived for more than a generation, can only appear as a fall from grace to a nation that has enjoyed an almost uniquely benign security experience during most of its history. Given formal sanction in the 1972 agreements with the Soviet Union, mutual deterrence means that this nation is a hostage to the power and intentions of the Soviet Union, just as the Soviet Union is a hostage to the power and intentions of the United States. This ultimate reliance on mutual threat at the price of mutual vulnerability is not only "a sad commentary on the human condition," as Mr. Reagan has noted, it is a state any government would aspire to escape, given the possible means of doing so, and particularly the government of a nation that has had our remarkable history of freedom from insecurity.

The evident attractions of transcending deterrence, and particularly through the same means that led us into deterrence, need not be labored. At the same time, these attractions will vary considerably not simply because of varying estimates of the possibilities held out by technology but also because of varying views entertained of the adversary. Moreover, the views entertained of the adversary will inevitably influence estimates made of the possibilities held out by technology. Here, as elsewhere, necessity—real or perceived—is the mother of hope, if not of invention. Those who view the Soviet Union as not only unalterably committed to expansion, but willing to run considerable risks and—if need be—to pay a considerable price for its expansionist goals, will take a quite different position on deterrence than those who entertain a more optimistic view of the Soviet regime and its foreign policy. The importance of seeing deterrence, and the disputes over deterrence, as much in political as in technical terms is apparent. So too, the importance of seeing the dispute over the prospects of transcending deterrence in a similar manner should be apparent. In this dispute, the technological optimists are almost invariably political pessimists, while the political optimists are in turn almost invariably technological pessimists.

The Reagan administration is clearly made up of the former. As such, it is an administration that has placed its hopes in technology rather than in politics. It is not difficult to understand why it has done so. Whereas technology appears as a possible way out of the nuclear dilemma that may be taken independent of the will and desire of the adversary, politics, and thus deterrence, are dependent on this will and desire. In this view, it is the mutuality of politics, and of deterrence, that is the besetting vice of both, just as it is the nonreciprocal character of the technological quest that is its great virtue.

In proclaiming their new strategic concept, Reagan administration officials have also seen fit to defend it by promoting a particular view of the deterrent relationship of the past generation. In this view, the relationship of mutual deterrence was entered into more as a matter of choice than of necessity. Until the early 1960s, it holds, there was no mutual deterrence, largely because we continued to invest large sums for strategic defense (at the time, against Soviet strategic bombers). Then the change, and the fateful choice, came. The administration's Secretary of Defense, Caspar Weinberger, has given this account:

> It was not until the Kennedy and Johnson administrations that we began to abandon our efforts to defend against nuclear attack, and instead base our entire security on the odd theory that you are safe only if you have no defense whatsoever. It came to be known as mutual assured destruction, or MAD. It has played a central role in the U.S. approach to arms control for the past 20 years; even though for many years now, actual U.S. strategy has

adjusted to the fact that the original MAD concept was flawed.
Our strategy . . . now seeks to avoid the targeting of populations.[5]

In accepting mutual deterrence, a White House publication
on the President's Strategic Defense Initiative reads:

> We accepted the notion that if both we and the Soviet Union were
> able to retaliate with devastating power even after absorbing a
> first strike, that stable deterrence would endure. That rather
> novel concept seemed at the time to be sensible for two reasons.
> First, the Soviets stated that they believed that both sides should
> have roughly equal forces and neither side should seek to alter
> the balance to gain unilateral advantage. Second, there did not
> seem to be any alternative. The state of the art in defensive sys-
> tems did not permit an effective defensive system. Today both of
> these basic assumptions are being called into question.[6]

The oddity or novelty of mutual deterrence through the
threat of retaliation, however, did not stem in the first place
from any theory or concept but from the nature of nuclear
weapons. Mutual deterrence was a condition before it was a
policy. The reality and compelling character of that condition
was made apparent at least as early as the 1962 Cuban missile
crisis. The meaning of the crisis was not that it precluded choice
but that it made certain choices—including the use of conventional arms—increasingly difficult because of the consequences
to which they might lead. It made them increasingly difficult
despite our possession at the time of strategic superiority.

Mutual deterrence through the threat of retaliation became
a policy not by choice but by necessity. Once imposed, efforts
were directed to making this necessity as safe and reliable as
possible. How this might best be done gave rise to differences

5. Quoted from *The Wall Street Journal*, January 2, 1985, p. 18. Excerpts of a
speech by Defense Secretary Caspar Weinberger to the Foreign Press Center in
Washington, D.C., on December 19, 1985.

6. Quoted from *The New York Times*, January 4, 1985, p. 8. Excerpts from a
pamphlet entitled, "The President's Strategic Defense Initiative."

that remain today unresolved. The idea of mutual assured destruction provided one answer. Readily caricatured, if only by virtue of its acronym MAD, and clearly startling in its implications, it nevertheless expressed the crux of the nuclear predicament, which was nothing other than the inordinate destructiveness of nuclear weapons and the apparent impossibility of mounting an effective defense against them. In these circumstances, the reasoning went, wisdom consisted in making a virtue out of the nuclear vice by pursuing arrangements which would insure that the use of nuclear weapons resulted in the common ruin of the attacked and the attacker. Given the then inaccuracy of missiles, this meant a level of industrial and civilian destruction (cities) that would evidently prove unacceptable to either side. And given the state of defensive technology, it meant that efforts at defense would prove ineffective, at best, and destabilizing, at worst, because of the illusions and fears they might encourage.

Mutual assured destruction was the latest version of the very old idea that war would disappear once its destructiveness promised to become sufficiently great. It was not the officials of the Kennedy and Johnson administrations who gave us this allegedly novel concept but a succession of eighteenth- and nineteenth-century thinkers who were persuaded that advances in the technology of war must ultimately do away with war altogether by making it too destructive. This same persuasion was voiced from the outset of the nuclear age. Indeed, the once most widely quoted expression of this theme came not from a visionary—or from a technocratic American Secretary of Defense—but from one of the century's greatest practitioners of statecraft, Winston Churchill, who remarked on the effect of nuclear weapons: "It may well be that we shall, by a process of sublime irony, have reached a stage in this story where safety will be the sturdy child of terror, and survival the twin brother of annihilation."[7]

---

7. In his essay on militarism in the eighteenth century Hans Speier notes that many writers of the period looked forward to the day when military science would result in putting an end to war. *Social Order and the Risks of War* (New York: George W. Steward, 1952), pp. 240–41. And John U. Nef has examined the view that arose in the seventeenth and eighteenth centuries to the effect that advances in the technology of war represent progress toward the eventual disap-

Has the evolution of weapons and strategy that has occurred since the 1960s overturned the essential premise of mutual assured destruction? American strategy no longer rests, and for many years has not rested, on the targeting of centers of population. But it does perforce continue to rest on the pervasive uncertainty attending any nuclear conflict between the superpowers. The various innovations in strategic doctrine—from "nuclear options" through "countervailing" to "prevailing"—have not affected this uncertainty over whether any meaningful limits can be placed on the use of nuclear weapons. Nor has this uncertainty been affected to any significant degree by the many refinements in nuclear weapons. What these developments have done is to convert a former assurance of mutual suicide—which critics insisted was never credible—into a present uncertainty of one—which supporters insist is tantamount to an assurance.

The difference between the mutual assured destruction of the mid 1960s and the mutual deterrence of today is accordingly a difference of degree rather than of kind. The vision of apocalypse has been slighty blurred, but it is still very much apparent. Deterrence rests today on the complete absence of assurance that any meaningful limits can be placed on the conduct of a nuclear war between the superpowers. In theory, that is quite different from the kind of assurance required by the doctrine of assured destruction. But this latter assurance could never be satisfactorily provided in any event, as critics of assured destruction were tireless in pointing out. In practice, then, the difference is one between the certainty of assurance and the

pearance of war. "This new thesis rested mainly on two arguments which are to some extent complementary. The first was put by Gibbon in classic form. The invention of powerful weapons is possible only when the level of civilization is raised, and the more civilized individuals and nations become, the less they are disposed to let force be the final arbiter of their destiny. The second argument is that powerful weapons are capable of such frightful destruction that they will bring a war to a speedy end, or even cause the leaders of the nations to recoil from war altogether." *War and Human Progress* (Cambridge: Harvard University Press, 1950), p. 200. This outlook persists throughout the nineteenth century and into the present century. Its persistence is a remarkable tribute to man's ingrained optimism that technology is, after all, a beneficent force.

assurance of uncertainty. If this difference ought not to be simply discounted, neither ought it to be exaggerated.

The persisting attack by the administration and its supporters on mutual assured destruction should be seen as a not so veiled attack on the present system of deterrence. It is the deep-rooted unhappiness with this system and the ever growing lack of faith in its effectiveness that have given rise to the insistence today that it not only be substantially altered but ultimately transcended. The mutual deterrence we have lived under for a generation, the now familiar indictment runs, has not worked in the manner promised by its architects. Over the past decade, the Soviet Union has not aimed at a rough equality of strategic forces but has sought to obtain strategic advantage. It has done so by its unrelenting buildup of land missiles, which now threatens the American land based missiles, just as it has done so by its clandestine attempts to escape the constraints laid down in the 1972 ABM agreement. As a result of these actions, the Soviet Union is now in a position where it may one day abandon even the pretense of seeking only strategic equality.

In this view, the failure of mutual deterrence and of concomitant efforts at arms control, are not primarily the result of technical misjudgement—though this played a role—but of political misjudgement. Mutual deterrence, along with the arms control agreements entered into in its name, depended centrally on a certain assessment of the party with whom we would entertain this relationship. It is now apparent, as it should have been apparent from the outset, that this assessment was badly in error. And it was badly in error because of the nature of the Soviet regime and, to a lesser though still important degree, because of the nature of democracies. What a critic says of the promise—or rather the threat—of arms control might almost as well be said of the larger relationship of mutual deterrence within which arms control efforts have been pursued. "The Soviet Union will sign arms-control agreements with the West only if such agreements are consistent with its fundamental political objectives—that is, only if they contribute to the extension of Soviet power and influence, normally at the direct expense of the West."[8] And in entering those agreements, he adds, democracies, instead of maintaining an alert and vigilant position, will almost invariably be lulled into a false sense of security.[9]

This indictment of arms control and, in effect, of mutual deterrence, can have little if any appeal, however, given its pervasive political pessimism. What the promise of the Strategic Defense Initiative has done is to redress this pessimism by holding out the prospect of escaping its consequences. In the short term, the initiative promises, technology can deliver us from the immediate perils of vulnerability by strengthening a now defective system of mutual deterrence. It can do so through a point defense of missile sites. In the long run, technology can enable us to escape altogether from the present system of deterrence.

Although it is the prospect of enhancing deterrence that is of immediate strategic significance, it is the promise of transcending the age of deterrence that makes up the political appeal of the defense initiative. The world this program looks to is not one in which faith in deterrence is restored but one in which there is no longer a need to restore faith. In this world, the deterrence of today will be replaced by a new relationship, and while it too may be termed deterrence—there is already the insistence of supporters on doing so—this deterrence of tomorrow will have an altogether different meaning and significance from the deterrence of yesterday and today. It is tempting to say that the new deterrence the administration's defense initiative ultimately holds out is indicative of a relationship that, were it to be once realized, is entirely reminiscent of an earlier and "normal" age. But this would not be true. For while the deterrence of yesterday and today is a sword—an annihilating sword—without a shield, the deterrence of tomorrow will presumably be a shield without a sword. The present deterrence threatens an

---

8. Seymour Weiss, "The Case Against Arms Control," *Commentary* (November 1984), p. 21.

9. "Arms control is certainly politically popular, but it is just as certainly the repository of false and dangerous hopes." Seymour Weiss, "The Case Against Arms Control," p. 23.

aggressor with terrible retaliation should he once resort to aggression. The future deterrence, we are told, threatens an aggressor with no punishment at all. "Our goal," Secretary Weinberger has stated, "is to destroy weapons that kill people."[10] The other and better means of deterring war, President Reagan has said of his initiative, "[is] by means other than threatening devastation to any aggressor—and by a means which threatens no one."[11]

If this is indeed the guiding vision behind the new strategic concept, the deterrence of tomorrow is not only novel but represents a greater break from past experience than the deterrence under which we now live. For the deterrence under which we now live at least preserves this continuity with the past: it rests on a social principle, reciprocity, that has nearly always been the most reliable in setting restraints on man's collective behavior. It breaks with the past not in carrying but in threatening to carry this principle to an extreme limit. The deterrence under which we presumably will live, however, has no apparent continuity with the past. While holding out the prospect of disarming an aggressor, it does so for no ostensible purpose other than defense. The destruction of the aggressor's weapons is not a step preparatory to the imposition of one's will. Instead, it is presented as a measure that constitutes an end in itself, and this despite the fact that it will have been taken to ward off an annihilating act of aggression. Whatever technological doubts the administration's new strategy must raise, they are surely no greater than the political skepticism it must provoke.

Can the promise of the Strategic Defense Initiative be realized? That promise, we need to remind ourselves, is twofold. The nearer prospect held out is the enhancement of the present system of mutual deterrence by the development of a terminal phase defense of point targets (primarily missile sites). The

---

10. See note 5 above.
11. See note 1 above.

more distant and far greater prospect is not the mere enhancement of the present system of deterrence but its transcendence
through the development of a comprehensive defense against
Soviet ballistic missiles. A comprehensive defense would protect populations, certainly our own and, it is even promised, our
allies' as well.

It is not the prospect of terminal phase or point defense that
is of interest here. Forbidden by treaty in 1972, one limited exception apart, terminal defense is restricted to the most accessi-
ble phase of an attacking missile's trajectory. To prove successful
in the defense of missile emplacement, the effectiveness of terminal defense need be no more than modest, since all that is
required is that a substantial portion of the missiles be saved.
This is in sharp contrast to the requirements of a comprehensive
system of defense that is intended for the protection of populations as well.

The central difficulty in devising a comprehensive system of
defense against ballistic missiles has been stated many times. It
is rooted in the very great destructiveness of nuclear weapons
and, to a lesser degree, the very great speed of ballistic missiles.
These characteristics have given the offense a predominance
that it has never before achieved. That predominance,
moreover, has seemed assured by the relative ease with which
simple and cheap countermeasures may be taken to defeat defensive efforts. Then, too, the requirements for "success" in the
case of defensive systems are far more exacting than are those of
offensive systems. Once again, this striking disproportionality is
due to the very great destructiveness of nuclear weapons.

Given this destructiveness, it will not be enough to destroy
a substantial percentage of ballistic missiles. Instead, an over-
whelming percentage of missiles must be destroyed. A defensive system that cannot come reasonably close to perfection may
greatly enhance deterrence but it cannot open the way to transcending the present system of deterrence. And even if a defense against ballistic missiles were developed that came close to
complete effectiveness, it would not result in transcending the
present system of deterrence unless it also had the capability of
defending against air breathing conveyances (aircraft, cruise
missiles, etc.) as well. For without the latter capability, we will

not have escaped from the nuclear threat. The time in which that threat might be carried out if only air breathing conveyances remained would possibly have been increased from minutes to hours. But this prospect is still a far cry from the prospect of a nuclear-free world.

To this forbidding set of requirements must be added still others. Even if a comprehensive defense against missiles and air breathing conveyances proved to be technologically possible, it would make no sense to deploy it unless it could survive attack and could be built as inexpensively as an adversary's counter measures. A defense system that was vulnerable to preemptive attack, the administration's senior advisor on arms control has emphasized, would constitute a tempting target for a first strike and, for this reason, would decrease stability rather than enhance it. In addition, a defense system that was not "cost effective at the margin, that is . . . cheap enough to add additional defensive capability so that the other side has no incentive to add additional offensive capability to overcome the defense," would constitute a steady drain on resources to no purpose.[12]

Is it reasonable to believe that these requirements might be met and the ultimate goal of the Strategic Defense Initiative attained? Even a decade ago, the answer was clearly a negative one. Today, SDI proponents argue, new technologies have brought within the realm of the possible what was once rightly deemed impossible. It is the proposal of a layered defense, along with the prospects entertained of each layer, that forms the principal basis of hope for the defense initiative. Supporters expect each layer to show an ever improving shift in the offense-defense cost-exchange ratio. But the most technically competent of former Secretaries of Defense has argued that "none of the proposed new layers of the SDI have been elaborated to the point where any significant calculation can be made to support such a claim. So far, the evidence is all to the contrary." And his own conclusion is that present technology does not offer even a "reasonable prospect" of a population defense.[13]

---

12. The senior advisor is Paul H. Nitze. His remarks quoted above were made in a February 20, 1985 speech to the Philadelphia World Affairs Council.

13. Quoted from an unpublished paper of Harold Brown, "The Strategic Defense Initiative: Defensive Systems and the Strategic Debate," February 1985.

Let us put aside the crucial issue that divides, and that will no doubt continue to divide, the scientists and engineers. Instead of asking whether the promise of SDI is attainable, we might instead ask whether it is desirable. Suppose that it were possible to realize the ultimate goal of the administration's defense initiative. What kind of world would this prospect hold out? Would we find it preferable to the world we have now?

The world we are imagining here is one in which nuclear weapons no longer play a role in the relations of the superpowers. They no longer do so because the United States and the Soviet Union have each managed to acquire an effective defense against not only ballistic missiles but air breathing conveyances as well. Moreover, these defensive systems have been effectively extended to the principal allies of each superpower.

A world where nuclear weapons no longer play a role[14] would therefore be a world where both space and airspace were no longer a usable medium for conducting war. The denial of the use of airspace for any strategic purposes would in effect reverse the principal development in warfare since the early part of this century. Unable to use the air as a medium of warfare, save perhaps tactically, we would move back to an age dominated again by land and naval forces. Of even greater importance, we would return to a world dominated by conventional balance of power calculations. Finally, we would largely restore our historic security position, for we would no longer be subject to the threat either of nuclear or even of conventional weapons carried by missiles or by aircraft.

It is, of course, the prospect of restoring something resembling our historic security that is the great attraction of the defense initiative. Would this undoubted benefit nevertheless be attended by certain disadvantages? In a post-nuclear world dominated once again by conventional balance of power calculations, would not the Soviet Union improve on its present position by virtue of its strength in conventional forces, unless the conventional forces of America and its Western European allies

---

14. Strictly speaking, this imaginary world would still be one where nuclear weapons played a role, since some of the smaller powers might still be expected to possess these weapons. Even so, this would likely have little if any effect on the relationship of the great powers.

were in turn strengthened? Most important of all, perhaps, is the effect of nuclear abolition on international stability. If the threat of nuclear war has been the principal reason for the stability of the present international system, would not the removal of this threat inaugurate a new period of greater instability?

These are the major issues that the prospect of a nuclear-free world must raise. Merely to raise them serves as a cautionary note to the assumption that transcending the present age of mutual deterrence would be an unmixed blessing. Still, it is difficult to find in them plausible reasons for believing that a post-nuclear world would not be markedly preferable to the present world. This is so even if it is granted that the return to a world governed by a balance of power might well improve the power position of the Soviet Union, particularly with respect to Western Europe. It might do so because the present imbalance of conventional forces there favorable to the Soviet Union is offset by the risk, and the fear, that a conventional conflict would end in the use of nuclear weapons. In a post-nuclear world, though, this restraint would no longer operate.

On this view, nuclear weapons have not only kept the peace, they have also inhibited the normal operation of the balance of power. With their disappearance, it is argued, the guarantee of peace we have enjoyed for the past four decades would also disappear. But even if it is granted that nuclear weapons have had these effects, the price we have paid for them has been quite high if only as measured by the loss of our historic security. More important, however, is the price that one day may have to be paid for them. It is only for those who believe the possibility of nuclear war to be altogether negligible that the price paid for these effects must appear quite reasonable. But for those who believe that so long as nuclear weapons remain in the armories of the superpowers the finite but very real possibility of nuclear war also remains, the price must seem high.

Besides, it is not written in the stars that in a post-nuclear world the nations of Western Europe and Japan must continue to remain dependent for their security on the United States. With the nuclear dimension once removed, they might make the effort in conventional forces that they have heretofore refused to make. They might do so because they would find a meaning and purpose in redressing a conventional imbalance that they do not find in a world governed by the nuclear balance of terror. Were they to do so, their material power might soon give them a role and salience in the new balance of power that would drastically alter the calculations we have become accustomed to making in the nuclear age. And in the new calculations, the role and salience of the Soviet Union might well be considerably reduced, since its material power would seem altogether manageable when arrayed against the resources of the United States and its major allies.

A world in which the threat of nuclear retaliation no longer played a role would still be far from a peaceful utopia; but only an obsessive conviction that any change from the present nuclear status quo must be a change for the worse will insist that even if the promise of SDI were attainable it would nevertheless be undesirable. Suppose, however, that the promise is not attainable. What might be the consequences of failure? Supporters of the defense initiative have the tendency to assume that there will be no serious consequences to be reckoned with should the effort fail. Their view is one of nothing ventured nothing gained, which is of course unexceptionable. But there is also the other side of this and it is that when much is ventured much may be lost.

There is, to begin with, the material cost of failure. Since this is the most apparent and the easiest measurement of cost, it is invariably the one that receives the most attention. But the material cost of failure may not prove to be the most important cost. If the defense initiative is abandoned after several years of research and development, the price tag of failure may still be very modest when viewed in relation to the present defense budget. Of course, to many opponents of the program, virtually any price tag that results in failure is too much. Their view is that since nothing can possibly be gained nothing should be ventured. Yet we cannot know that failure is foreordained. Besides, failure or success here is not so simple and clear cut as opponents regularly assume. The initiative comprises at least two objectives. If only the first, and more limited, of these objectives is met, the program may be judged a failure when measured by its second, and more ambitious, promise, but it will nevertheless have accomplished something. Whether this more modest accomplishment might have been reached by alternative and less costly means, that is, by arms control, or whether it was even necessary to reach it at all, are questions that would no doubt persist. Even so, they do not affect the point that judgements of success or failure in terms of material cost may prove to be anything but unambiguous.

There are other costs to be reckoned, however, and though they are less objective they may be more important. An effort that issues in partial success, though failing to realize the promise of a population defense, may enhance the system of deterrence under which we now live. Nevertheless, this enhancement might be attended by the further erosion of the public's faith in this system of deterrence. It is not so much the enhancement of today's mutual deterrence that can arouse public hopes and expectations, but the promise of escaping altogether from the balance of terror. Admittedly, these hopes and expectations are as yet quite modest. In time, however, they may be expected to grow in response to government efforts to elicit support for its program. This support cannot but be bought at the price of a further erosion of faith in deterrence. For the logic of the administration's position requires it to elicit public support for the defense initiative by continuing to cast doubts on the efficiency and reliability of the present system of deterrence. A process of delegitimizing mutual deterrence appears as almost the unavoidable consequence of the endeavor to move beyond it. How far this delegitimization may go remains an open question. The process itself does not.

Uncertainty is yet another cost of the defense initiative. It is a cost whether the program issues in success or in failure. Critics of SDI have made a great deal of the cost. They have pointed out that uncertainty is the enemy of stability. A long period of uncertainty, they have argued, is bound to result in a prolonged and even dangerous instability. This instability will presumably attend the years of research and development before it is known whether a full-scale defense is technologically and economically feasible. But it is seen as particularly apparent and dangerous during the period of actual deployment unless both sides manage to deploy at roughly the same time and in a political environment marked by a far greater degree of trust and good will than has been evident in recent years.

The administration's response to the perils of uncertainty and instability likely to attend the defense initiative has largely been one of assuming circumstances that would evidently avoid these perils. The difficulty with the response has consisted in the unlikelihood of the assumptions made. Once it was assumed that uncertainty might be avoided, and the Soviet Union assured of the future, by our promise to share with it the results of our effort. Initially made by the President, this unprecedented offer has since been put aside. Its place has been taken by the assumption that the Soviet Union would deploy a defensive system of roughly comparable effectiveness at approximately the same time.[15]

Even if this latter assumption were to be credited, the great transition from the present world of offense to the future world of defense could prove quite complex and difficult. For there is bound to come a point in this transition where the balance between offensive and defensive weapons becomes very delicate and the apprehensions of each side mount. Should these apprehensions not be moderated at the time by a more relaxed relationship with the Soviet Union than the one we have today, the resulting situation could prove precarious. It must prove far more precarious, though, if, as is more likely, the administration's assumption of "parallel deployments" is misplaced and the Soviet Union trailed us by a number of years in deploying a similar defense system. In that event, Moscow would be confronted with the prospect that has so frightened the administration: the unilateral deployment of an effective defense. If that were to happen, administration officials have contended, deterrence would collapse and, in the words of a White House document, "we would have no choices between surrender and suicide." It would not be surprising if Soviet officials were to

---

15. "Should it prove possible to develop a highly capable defense against ballistic missiles, we would envision parallel United States and Soviet deployment, with the outcome being enhanced mutual security and international stability." "The President's Strategic Defense Initiative," p. 4.

take a similar view of their prospects in contemplating our unilateral deployment of an effective defense.

The uncertainties likely to attend the research, development and deployment of a comprehensive system of defense may eventually be surmounted. But even if we suppose
that they are and that success caps the efforts of the Strategic
Defense Initiative, we cannot suppose that no uncertainty will
then remain. For it is clear that in this event the greatest uncertainty of all must remain. Even if a system is developed and
deployed that in theory and design comes very close to complete effectiveness, there will remain the residual uncertainty
attending its operation. There is no reason to assume that this
uncertainty would be any less profound and any less troubling
than the uncertainty that has always attended the issue of
whether meaningful limits can be placed on the use of nuclear
weapons. In the absence of putting the matter to a test, we
cannot know. Yet a test may prove fatal. So too, we cannot know
whether a defense system will prove effective—particularly one
that is extraordinarily complex and dependent on several new
technologies—short of putting it to a test that may prove fatal.
This being the case, a successful defense initiative will not have
succeeded in resolving the terrible uncertainty created by nuclear weapons, thereby transcending the present system of deterrence, but have added yet another uncertainty to that which
already confronts us.

What the believers in the administration's defense initiative
have failed to see is that there is no apparent way of reliably
lifting the great uncertainty resulting from nuclear weapons
through technological means alone. But if technology cannot
give the assurance many nevertheless demand of it, can we get
such assurance from politics? There is one policy that might, if
adopted, go a long way toward conferring the kind of assurance
many seek from technology. Moreover, like the technological
quest, it has the attraction that it may be pursued independent
of the will and desire of the Soviet Union (or of allies).

A policy of withdrawal represents another possible way of attempting to escape from the nuclear dilemma. It is quite true that a policy of withdrawal could not result in the transcendence of the present system of deterrence. No matter how thoroughgoing and how successful that policy, it would nevertheless leave mutual deterrence intact. Even so, the significance of mutual deterrence would be profoundly altered, since whatever the prospects of nuclear war today, they would be reduced to a still lower order of magnitude. In this respect, at any rate, withdrawal does not suffer by comparison with the attempt to escape the present system of deterrence by way of the technical fix, since technology as well does not permit such escape.

The nuclear logic of a policy of withdrawal is simple enough. If the interests in defense of which we were prepared to risk not only nuclear war but any serious use of force did not extend beyond the North American continent, the prospect of our future involvement in a nuclear conflict would sharply decline. It would sharply decline because deterrence, having now become synonymous with the prevention of a direct attack by the Soviet Union upon the United States, would possess maximum credibility. It would do so even assuming that the Soviet Union's strategic forces enjoyed a substantial advantage over our own forces. For the Soviet Union would still have to incur terrible risks in attacking this country. In a world where we would no longer contest them, what incentive would the Soviets have to take such risks? An America, then, that defined its vital interests in terms that did not extend beyond this continent would be an America that placed its physical security in least jeopardy. By the same token, it would also be an America that was freed of much of the present nuclear uncertainty.

This, at least, is the principal thrust the argument on behalf of a policy of withdrawal must take. It remains the case, however, that the argument on behalf of withdrawal is one that has yet to receive much open support. Even among those who are most adamant about the dangers of our present nuclear strategy and most insistent upon changing that strategy, there is an unwillingness to draw the connection, or even to acknowledge a connection, between a policy of withdrawal and a radical change in nuclear strategy. It may be that withdrawal is nevertheless the unavowed agenda of much of the anti-nuclear weapons movement. Certainly, this is the conclusion one is almost driven to make in the case of some of its most articulate supporters. It may also be, however, that in the case of many—perhaps the majority—we have the not unfamiliar situation of a movement that entertains contradictory goals, that seeks to change substantially, and in time even radically, the nation's nuclear strategy while not changing in any significant way the nation's interests and commitments. In this instance, moreover, the ground for entertaining goals all too likely to prove incompatible, has been well prepared by arguments on behalf of the compatibility between radical change in nuclear strategy and continuity in major interests of postwar policy.[16]

The infrequency with which a policy of withdrawal is given serious consideration today must no doubt be found in the legacy of our interwar experience. Then, a policy of withdrawal—of isolation—principally from Europe, threatened in the end to lead to the worst of outcomes. The persisting fear that it would do so again must in large measure account for the near unanimity with which the undesirability of withdrawal is still considered to keep it beyond the pale of serious discussion.

If withdrawal is unthinkable, though, the reasons for this ought at least to be made clear. Certainly, it will not do to respond that the unthinkable may not be thought else it would become thinkable. Walter Lippmann once pointed out that this

---

16. It is not only the peace movement that affords grounds for skepticism about its ultimate—if unavowed—objectives. Skepticism also arises with respect to the outlook of the administration—or, at any rate, with respect to the outlook of a part of the Reagan administration. Although it outwardly rejects anything resembling a return to the past, the persistence of traits reminiscent of an isolationist past has been apparent from the outset of this administration's tenure in office. A marked impatience with allies has been one sign of this, as has a brief flirtation with what was dubbed a policy of "global unilateralism"—that is, a policy of progressive detachment from Europe attended by a policy of active involvement elsewhere. While nothing came of this expression of growing disenchantment with European allies, it served as a reminder of the persistence of an isolationist outlook. For what was appealing about global unilateralism was not so much its globalism as its unilateralism—the prospect of once again "going it alone" in the world. In some measure, the Strategic Defense Initiative must also provoke fears among allies of an isolationist resurgence.

reasoning was part of the case made against alliances and he argued that an objection which men would not examine and debate was a mere prejudice. In part, the case against withdrawal is also little more than a prejudice.

In part, however, this case rests on the assumption that even if we were once to decide upon a policy of withdrawal, we would do so only subsequently to find ourselves forced to try to retrace our steps in circumstances more dangerous to our security than ever. Suppose, it may be argued, that we were to withdraw from Europe only to attempt to return in circumstances of great instability, brought on by Soviet threats to forestall nuclear arming by West Germany. Clearly, this would be a very dangerous situation and it would have been largely brought on by our withdrawal.

It may well be objected that this argument succeeds by juxtaposing very nearly the worst of possible worlds, resulting from our decision to withdraw, with something resembling if not the best then a very tolerable world, resulting from our determination to retain the present policy. Still, it is not unreasonable to put a greater burden on those moving for radical change in policy. An American withdrawal, however staged, would be a momentous event. The uncertainties that it would open up are considerably greater than the uncertainties attendant upon a policy of the status quo.

The relevant question here, however, is whether the instability arising from our withdrawal would represent a greater threat to our core security than the continued pursuit of the policy of extended deterrence. The argument that withdrawal would represent a greater threat rests on the assumption that we would not—indeed, could not—accept the consequences of withdrawal. This unwillingness—and inability—to accept the consequences of our decision, it is argued, could easily result in something near the worst of possible worlds. And well it could. But this world would threaten our physical security only if having decided for other reasons that we could not live with the consequences we determined to retrace our steps.

What are these other reasons that would presumably drive us to retrace our steps? One, many would insist, is the very prospect of a war again occurring in Europe, a war we could not escape involvement in, just as we could not escape involvement in World Wars I and II. But one compelling reason why we could not avoid intervening in previous wars was because of balance of power considerations. A hostile power in control of Europe, we calculated, might ultimately pose a threat to our physical security. The calculation may have involved an element of exaggeration. Still, it was not unreasonable, resting as it did on the assumption that the power of this nation might not prove sufficient to deter attack by a hostile power in control of Europe, or even worse, Eurasia.

This reasoning, though, seems no longer relevant. It applied to a pre-nuclear world and to a balance of power system. In such a system a surfeit of defensive and deterrent power was practically unachievable. This being so, a great object of diplomacy was to avoid isolation. In this respect, as in so many others, nuclear-missile weapons have effected a revolution in international politics. A great nuclear state, able to destroy any other state or combination of states, is no longer dependent on balance of power considerations for its core security. It possesses what was heretofore considered unachievable: a surfeit of deterrent power. And although in the extreme situation it is absolutely vulnerable with respect to its great nuclear adversary, this vulnerability cannot be significantly affected by alliances and allies. On the contrary, while allies cannot improve one's core security they may threaten it, since the prospect of using nuclear weapons is most likely to arise as a result of threats to their security.

These considerations do not address the argument that a nuclear peace is indivisible and that we cannot escape our present involvement in Europe if only for the simple yet compelling reason that a nuclear conflict in Europe would inevitably become a global nuclear conflict. This argument is of a piece with the view, also put forth with utter assurance, that any use of nuclear weapons between the great powers must result in the unlimited use of nuclear weapons between them. Still, the latter view has at least something more to support it than mere assertion, although ultimately it too is necessarily speculative. The former view, however, seems no more than mere assertion. Far from being of necessity indivisible, a nuclear peace may be more divisible than any peace we have known for a very long time. Why must a policy of involvement that requires extended deterrence be defended by arguments that no longer carry persuasion? It is as though those making them fear that if the truth were known about why we persist in such policy it might prove insufficient to command the necessary support. The truth is scarcely startling. If we refuse to equate our vital interests simply with our physical security, it is because great nations have almost always refused to make this equation. They have always insisted that their identity consists of more than physical attributes and that it encompasses the preservation of certain values and of the institutions—political, economic, and social—that embody these values. Nations require allies and friends not only for reasons of physical security but in order to insure an environment that will be receptive to these values. In the end, this is why we have refused to entertain a policy of withdrawal, even though this continued refusal may one day exact a terrible price.

The Strategic Defense Initiative in its more ambitious dimensions and a policy of withdrawal represent two ways of attempting to escape from the present system of deterrence. What informs them both is the conviction that it is neither possible nor desirable to restore a former faith in this system. By contrast, the attempt to regain a position of strategic superiority may be seen as an attempt to recreate the circumstances that once conditioned the operation of faith. The critical circumstance, of course, was the position of strategic superiority this country enjoyed over the Soviet Union. In retrospect, there is now a tendency to discount the view that strategic superiority once conferred real and significant advantages. The fashionable theme of the inherent disutility of nuclear weapons is applied to a recent past in order to correct the presumably mistaken view that our strategic position ever operated to our advantage. If it did not, then the attempt today to recapture some semblance of strategic advantage must be regarded as at best a vain enterprise, and this even if there were a reasonable prospect that the effort might one day succeed. This nuclear revisionism notwithstanding, the strategic superiority of yesterday did confer advantages. Not the least of these advantages was a degree of faith in the operation of deterrence that has since declined. Whether this faith might be restored to a former level, even if a measure of strategic superiority were once regained, is surely a legitimate question. But it cannot be answered simply by tendentious readings of the past that are sharply at variance with common-sense interpretations. Nor can it be fairly responded to by intimations to the effect that the very attempt to regain a measure of strategic advantage over the Soviet Union must be regarded as inherently undesirable and even as illegitimate. The attempt may prove impossible to achieve, and even if possible it may have undesirable consequences that outweigh the benefits of superiority. But these are different matters. To judge it as inherently undesirable and even as illegitimate, if only for the reason that the Soviet Union might consider the effort synonymous with a policy of confrontation, is to sanction the disadvantages under which our position of extended deterrence must operate in conditions approximating strategic parity.

The promise of technology has once again stimulated hopes of regaining some semblance of strategic advantage. It has done so with respect to the precision guided munitions. The advent of offensive weapons of great accuracy would evidently confer a substantial measure of strategic advantage if, being largely in the possession of one side, they had a highly effective counterforce capability. But the history of the past three decades does not afford much reason for assuming that the lead we may presently enjoy in precision guided munitions will be kept for more than a brief period. Nor is there much reason to assume that the effectiveness of these weapons as a counterforce system will be greater in our hands than in Soviet hands. If anything, it is the contrary assumption that seems more reasonable. For the differences between the two societies must make the concealment of targets appropriate to the new weapons far more difficult for the United States than for the Soviet Union. The openness of American society almost ensures that as between the two we would be the disadvantaged party. Would the development of an effective defense of fixed points, or of limited areas, confer a strategic advantage? It is difficult to see how it might do so, particularly if we assume that the Soviet Union would not simply remain passive during the period of our development. A point defense might serve to enhance deterrence by ensuring the retaliatory capability of our land based ICBMs. It might close once and for all the notorious "window of vulnerability" that was presumably opened in the 1970s with the appearance of Soviet land based missiles capable of destroying American land based missiles. But this renewal of the retaliatory capability of our land based missiles would not of itself confer a strategic advantage. It might confer such advantage—or, at least, some have argued—if joined to new weapons systems that could in turn put the Soviet land based deterrent at risk by posing a credible first strike capability. In the course of the coming decade, such weapons systems will indeed become operational (the land based MX missile, the Trident submarine with its highly accurate D-5 missile, etc.). But even with these new weapons systems, the United States will be in approximately the position that the Soviet Union has presumably been in since the late 1970s. That position has not been one of superiority. It has not even been one of marked advantage, and the Soviet Union has neither claimed the contrary not acted as the superior or advantaged party. And, of course, all this assumes the Soviet government would be idly standing by during this period, rather than undertaking to place in operation effective terminal phase defense of its own.

It is increasingly apparent that the period formally inaugurated by the 1972 ABM treaty is rapidly drawing to a close and will be succeeded by the growing unwillingness of the great nuclear powers to forego defensive efforts. But these efforts are unlikely to restore strategic superiority. They might do so if we were not only to move well ahead but to remain well ahead of the Soviet Union in the competition to develop a comprehensive missile defense. The assumption that we can remain well ahead is rooted in the belief that is as old as the postwar competition in arms between the United States and the Soviet Union. In this view, the Soviet Union is and will remain the technological inferior of this country. Yet our superiority has not prevented the inferior party from duplicating our technological achievements in weapons and often within a very brief period. On more than one occasion, this duplication has also been carried out with a vengeance. There is no apparent reason to conclude that on this occasion the Soviet Union would prove unable to do what it has done in the past. Having sacrificed so much to reach its present position of strategic eminence, it may be expected to remain willing to make the necessary effort and sacrifice to keep this position.

It would be ironic if the principal consequence of defensive efforts, rather than conferring a measure of strategic advantage, were instead to subject our principal alliance to new and serious strain. For the result of those efforts, despite assurances to the contrary, might be to create a system that differentiates between the defense of this country and the defense of Western Europe. The view has been expressed that in the event of a two class system of defense, Europe would intensify its perennial fear of the United States decoupling from its allies. But surely it would not be our growing invulnerability to Soviet missile attack that heightened this fear. A growing invulnerability, however modest, should instead reassure our allies, on the reasoning that what promotes American strategic invulnerability strengthens extended deterrence. On this reasoning, the Europeans should welcome America's growing invulnerability. Admittedly, a growing Soviet invulnerability as well must partly offset this reassurance to Western Europe. Still, the net result, one might think, would still point to Western European reassurance.

In all likelihood, though, the reality would be otherwise and would result from Western Europe's perception that it was now more exposed than ever. The fact that the two great nuclear adversaries were increasingly protected, while Europe was not, would heighten fears that the risks of nuclear war *in Europe* had increased, that in the words of a former mayor of West Berlin, Heinrich Albertz, Europe was now being turned into a "shooting gallery of the superpowers." However unfounded the perception, it might nevertheless be broadly shared. For it would reflect the familiar "logic" of the protected that their security consists in there being no sanctuaries.

The prospect of regaining some semblance of strategic superiority is attractive not only for the advantages it is believed to entail but for the reason that it may be pursued independent of the will and desire of the Soviet Union. As such, it is to be sharply contrasted with the principal alternative, détente, which is evidently dependent on the cooperation of the Soviet Union. The attraction of détente as a way of restoring faith in deterrence is that it may prove more promising than the technical fix while less likely to result in the sacrifice of interest that withdrawal holds out.

If the view earlier expressed is correct, the immediate and decisive reason for the lapse of faith in deterrence at the beginning of the 1980s was the breakdown of détente. Unquestionably, the loss of strategic superiority affords the deeper explanation of the lapse. Yet it is remarkable that the passing of our strategic superiority had so limited an effect on both the general public and, more significantly, the foreign policy elites. The fact that it did not shake the faith that had been formed in an earlier period must be attributed largely to the relationship of détente that arose in the course of the middle to late 1960s, reached a high point in the early 1970s, and was already in marked decline by the middle 1970s. Although the tangible achievements of that relationship were quite modest, it nevertheless had a remarkably reassuring effect on the public and elites alike.

To the critics of this earlier experience with détente, however, it is precisely the reassuring effect it had that demonstrates the great danger held out in entering into yet another détente. For it was this sense of reassurance, they contend, that created the general context within which the strategic position of this country not only markedly declined relative to the Soviet Union but a dangerous vulnerability arose that we have yet to overcome. This vulnerability presumably results from the large number of Soviet land based missiles that can put to risk the American land missile force. The awareness of this vulnerability could one day tempt the Soviet leadership to pursue a dangerous course of action in the expectation that the American government, aware of the peril in which it was placed, would concede the issue in dispute rather than hazard a nuclear confrontation.

Given expression as early as 1976–77, the window of vulnerability argument was employed with considerable effect in the Reagan campaign of 1980. In the succeeding years, it has been moderated, though never abandoned. From the outset, it has been sharply contested as raising groundless fears over a retaliatory capability that is, and promises to remain, quite effective.

At bottom, the ensuing dispute has never turned primarily on the narrower technical considerations each side has advanced but on the assumptions each has made about the political utility of any marked asymmetry in strategic nuclear forces and, of course, the willingness of the Soviet government to exploit such asymmetries to achieve its expansionist goals. The view that the present disparity in land missile forces seriously threatens the stability of mutual deterrence evidently assumes that such disparity can be turned to political advantage and likely will be so turned by a government willing to run considerable risks in pursuit of its interests. But our experience to date does not afford much support for this view. What it does seem to show is that a position of overall strategic superiority can be used to effective advantage on behalf of essentially defensive interests. This is the apparent lesson of the Cuban missile crisis, though not a few continue to question its validity. Yet even if it is accepted without question, it can afford little, if any, support to the assumptions that have formed the basis of the window of vulnerability view. Nor is this view supported by the actions of the Soviet government during years when the window was if not open then opening. In the period from 1980 to 1985 Soviet behavior was as cautious and circumspect as it has ever been.

Finally, the Reagan administration has never quite behaved in a way that would give credence to its professed concern about the window of vulnerability. Although on coming to office it insisted that the Soviet land missile force held out grave danger to the American deterrent posture, once in office it allowed its response to these alleged dangers to be influenced by domestic political considerations. Thus it rejected the deceptive basing mode planned by the preceding Carter administration for the MX missile system, in part because it had made this basing mode an object of derision during the election and in part because influential supporters in Congress, reflecting views of constituents, objected to having the new system in their respective states. Instead, the administration began a rather leisurely search for a new basing mode, a search that after four years proved quite barren of results. It was a curious reaction to what was held up as a serious security threat.

The détente of the early 1970s can scarcely be held responsible for the impressive inadvertence shown in the handling of the MX missile system. Whether this détente should even be held responsible for the relative decline in the American strategic position that occurred in the preceding decade is itself a question that yields no simple answer. In part, at least, this decline was the inescapable result of a development that was independent of détente. The determination of the Soviet Union to achieve strategic parity, and our inability to prevent it from doing so, are rooted in conditions and circumstances that precede the 1972 détente and form the very essence of the great rivalry. In the 1960s, this determination was apparent, as was our initial adjustment to it. The détente of the 1970s carried forward a process that had already effected a profound change in the strategic relationship.

The détente of the past decade cannot be held accountable for change that in large measure would have come in any event. This must be said in view of the penchant today on the part of the right to make détente virtually synonymous with appeasement. The equation is unjustified. What, after all, does the experience of the 1970s show? It shows this: a détente that is concluded in inauspicious circumstances, that is flawed in design, that lacks adequate means for achieving the ends sought, that depends on too personalized a scheme of implementation, and that, finally, is badly oversold, is doomed to fail.

The Nixon-Kissinger détente was undertaken in a period of

declining American power. Entered into from a position of relative weakness, and in the dark shadows cast by a disastrous war in Vietnam, détente was to serve as the new version of containment. It reflected the basic conviction that the growth of Soviet power, when taken together with what was seen as a mounting reluctance at home to support a policy of global engagement, meant that American interests would have to be preserved through less taxing means than those employed in the past.

The principal question the 1972 détente raised was what would induce the Soviet Union to refrain in the future from exploiting opportunities and taking advantage of instabilities, particularly in the third world. In part, the answer given at the time was that in return for American recognition of the Soviet Union as a strategic equal, Moscow would accept American-inspired rules of the superpower competition. This assumed a Soviet Union increasingly committed to the status quo throughout the world. In part, Soviet good behavior was also to result from a combination of positive incentives—primarily economic in character. This assumed that Soviet high policy could be substantially influenced by economic inducements. Neither of these assumptions was easy to credit. The Soviet leaders had never indicated they were prepared to abandon their aspirations in the third world. To them, global parity meant, among other things, an equal right to play the game of *Weltpolitik*. We might still seek to dissuade them from asserting this right by holding out carrots. But economic means, whether in the form of pressures or inducements, had never influenced Soviet high policy in the past.

The positive incentives and diplomatic pressures of the 1972 détente did not hold out much promise of preventing the assertion of interests in the third world by the Soviets. Nor did the previous methods of containment. The policy of détente clearly did not accord to these methods the same role that they had previously played or there would have been little need for the new diplomatic design on which so much emphasis was placed. The previous methods of containment, after all, had given rise to the difficulties that the new design was supposed to alleviate. The assumption that if the means distinctive to the new design did not prove effective, the old methods might always be resorted to was plausible only if the old methods were somehow to be applied in a more daring and imaginative manner. The promise of détente depended, in the last analysis, on the virtuosity in the use of power displayed by President Nixon and his principal assistant. The policy was highly personalized, too personalized for the American democracy. When Watergate paralyzed and then destroyed the Nixon presidency, Henry Kissinger was left to implement détente and to do so in unfavorable circumstances. Far from acting restrained, the Soviet Union continued its arms buildup, supplied weapons and gave encouragement to the Arab states in the 1973 war, and intervened in southern Africa.

What are the lessons to be learned from the 1972 détente? Surely one is that the prospects for détente, any détente, are not promising when entered into from a position of weakness. The circumstances attending the détente of the past decade were such that the outcome was prejudiced from the start, and this was so even had the original architects been left at liberty to implement their diplomatic creation.

Another lesson is that the promise of détente is, at best, a limited one. At least, this would appear to be the case in the absence either of a truly multipolar world or of regime change in the Soviet Union. Given the persistence of the structural and ideological determinants of the Soviet-American conflict, even a quite successful détente can only be expected to affect the margins of the relationship. The promise of détente is not for that reason unimportant. But this promise cannot achieve the goals that presumably formed a part of the 1972 détente. Had the Soviet Union really undertaken the kind of abstentionist pledge that the American sponsors of détente insisted it had made in agreeing to the "basic principles" of the 1972 Moscow agreement, this would have signaled a fundamental change in Soviet policy. The result would have been no mere relaxation of tensions but a transformation of the underlying conflict. This is indeed how the 1972 détente was often represented. As such, it was to have been no mere détente, but a far-reaching understanding—an entente—that would have affected the fate of the entire world. The representation was misleading and could only have led to overblown expectations followed by disillusionment.

The experience of the 1970s also supports the view that so long as the essential factors conditioning the superpower relationship remain unchanged, the United States and the Soviet Union are doomed to permanent rivalry. Within the limits set by this rivalry their relationship may vary. But the variation, though not without significance, is unlikely to go beyond a relatively narrow range. Thus it is apparent that neither of the extreme alternatives for resolving conflicts is any longer open to the great rivals, or, for that matter, that anything even roughly approximating the alternatives of confrontation or condominium affords a feasible course of action.

A policy of confrontation would require a position of strategic superiority that neither side possesses today nor is likely to possess in the foreseeable future. Even when we enjoyed superiority we did not pursue a policy of confrontation, for we have never followed a policy that sought a favorable resolution of the conflict by forcing the Soviet Union to choose between war and the sacrifice of interests it regards as vital. Today, a confrontationist policy would be altogether lacking in credibility and both sides by their behavior show an awareness of this. Moreover, the American pursuit of a policy of confrontation would be strongly resisted by those on whose behalf it was presumably undertaken. Finally, it would go far beyond the present, or any likely future, domestic consensus on foreign policy.

Condominium, on the other hand, appears an even less likely prospect than confrontation. It seems an even less likely prospect not only because of the persisting basic dispositions of the superpowers but because the objects of competition between them are less passive today than they once were. Even in the late 1940s and 1950s, the world was surprisingly resistant to the superpowers. At present, the circumstances requisite for anything resembling a condominial arrangement are still less apparent. Indeed, the years marking the high point of détente in the 1970s showed that our allies are almost as apprehensive over and resistant to any comprehensive understanding between Washington and Moscow as they are over a relationship that even suggests confrontation.

These considerations do not rule out the prospect of a substantial moderation of the American-Soviet relationship. But if such moderation is to enjoy a happier fate than the 1970s détente, it will have to be attended by progress in reaching a political settlement of the several regional conflicts in which the United States and the Soviet Union have an interest. The outlook for this, however, is no better today than it has ever been. If anything, the superpowers now show less disposition to cooperative action in regional conflicts than they have shown in the past. Accordingly, these conflicts may be expected to remain a source of discord and not an opportunity for collaboration.

It may of course be argued that the promise of détente will instead depend largely on the prospect of reaching significant arms control agreements. For the considerations that made arms control the centerpiece of the old détente are all the more compelling today. Arms control apart, there is little else to give even symbolic, let alone, concrete, form to a marked reduction in tensions between Washington and Moscow. In the past decade, the public and its elites have come to accord arms control a central place in the superpower relationship. In part, this is to be explained by the character of nuclear weapons and the fears these weapons continue to generate. Then too, arms control appears as the only variable in an otherwise unchanging conflict, and thus as the principal basis for hope.

These developments may have made arms control agreements more important to reach; they have not made them any easier to reach. It is precisely because greater significance is given to arms control that the obstacles to progress seem, if anything, more imposing today. For the competitive energies the superpowers once invested in geographical conflicts of interest, they now increasingly invest in arms control. Unable to resolve their geographical conflicts through compromise, yet unwilling to take the risks unilateral action might impose, they have increasingly turned to arms control as the forum for carrying on their competition. The principal result has been to magnify the difficulties that would in any event attend arms control negotiations between two such adversaries.

The investing of arms control with a political significance it never before possessed explains why it is more apparent today than ever that an improved political relationship between the two superpowers is the precondition of virtually any significant measures of arms control. More than this, there is a rough proportionality that must be expected to hold between the state of this relationship and the prospects for arms control measures. A modestly improved relationship may create the basis for modest measures of arms control. This being the case, ambitious arms control schemes are either purely imaginary undertakings or they are predicated on a relationship between the United States and the Soviet Union that goes well beyond even a quite loose definition of détente. This is why proposals for very deep cuts in nuclear arms are idle unless they assume a relationship that has in all likelihood passed beyond the stage of a mere détente and has become something more intimate and promising. But the prospects for this are such that they seem scarcely worth pausing over.

What, then, are we to conclude? If a restoration of faith in deterrence depends upon marked change in the present relationship between the United States and the Soviet Union, together with the arms control measures that would presumably attend such change, it is unlikely that we will see any such restoration. It may be that a former faith in deterrence cannot be restored. Yet it may also be that a former faith need not be restored, that something more modest will do. A distinction must be drawn between restoring faith in deterrence, even if not a former faith, and reducing the risk of nuclear war. What the restoration of a faith of sorts requires may turn out to be something quite modest in the way of arms control. For this, a correspondingly modest détente may in turn prove sufficient.

Even so, a modest détente, with its attendant measures of arms control, will not prove easy. It will require the United States and the Soviet Union if not to abandon the use of arms control as a means for obtaining competitive advantage then at least to find in arms control an instrument of cooperation as well as of competition. At a time when so much of the conflict between the superpowers finds expression in the area of arms control, the expectation that they may yet consider a more balanced view of arms control to be in their mutual interest may seem out of place. If it is, the nuclear anxiety we have recently experienced can be expected to persist and indeed to deepen.

This conclusion will elicit the objection that it ignores the great issue at the heart of the nuclear debate today, which is the need to diminish the danger of nuclear war. For what is necessary to maintain a modest détente with the Soviet Union and to restore a faith in deterrence may still fall considerably short of what is necessary to reduce the risk of nuclear war. It is the latter, arms control supporters insistently remind us, that forms the great purpose of arms control. Thus a recent essay on the case for arms control reads: "The United States and the USSR bring one overriding shared objective to arms control negotiations: reducing the risk of nuclear war."[17]

Reducing the risk of nuclear war may be our overriding shared objective with the Soviet Union. But it is clearly not *our* overriding objective, or *theirs*, else it would be difficult to account for the persistence of the danger of nuclear war. If reducing this danger were the overriding objective of each power, each would long ago have agreed to measures that instead have been resisted. One reason for this resistance may be that the superpowers do not quite believe there is a finite risk of nuclear war, and this whatever American and Soviet leaders may say. Belief, as we know, is betrayed by a pattern of behavior consisting of small and seemingly inconsequential actions, yet actions

---

17. Barry M. Blechman, "The Case for Nuclear Arms Control," Working Paper No. 47, Center for International and Strategic Affairs, University of California, Los Angeles (January 1985), p. 4.

that are in their totality revealing. More than one perceptive observer has commented on the absence of such a pattern in the behavior of successive administrations.

For the most part, however, the reason for this resistance is simply that each superpower is willing to run the present risk of nuclear war rather than to sacrifice interests that each fears the substantial lowering, if not the removal, of this risk might entail. The shared interest in reducing the risk of nuclear war is subordinated to other and unshared interests. At least, this is the case in periods of normalcy. It is only in a period of great crisis that the normal hierarchy of interests can be expected to undergo an abrupt change. For if it cannot be so expected, the outcome of crisis will likely be nuclear war.

In considering the great purpose or objective of arms control, then, one must distinguish between normal times and crises. In a crisis, this objective of reducing the risk of nuclear war must prove far more compelling than in normal times. In a crisis, we can only assume that this overriding shared objective also becomes each side's overriding separate objective as well. And if this assumption expresses something more solid than hope, as we have reason to believe that it does, the risk of nuclear war may be considered virtually synonymous with the danger of miscalculation. It is the risk of miscalculation in severe crises that largely defines the residual risk of nuclear war.

Why this is so should be readily apparent. It is because of the common persuasion that, short of surrender, no outcome of a crisis, however grave, could be worse than initiating a nuclear war. This persuasion is a historical novelty in the literal sense. Its effect is to confine the prospects of war between the great powers within limits that are far narrower than they have ever been.

The objection may nevertheless be made that to find the residual risk of nuclear war in the danger of miscalculation is still to acknowledge a prospect that is far from negligible. After all, it may be said of most wars that they are the result of miscalculation. Save for the nihilist, the party that initiates a war that is subsequently lost has evidently miscalculated. The history of state relations is in significant measure the history of wars that are the result of miscalculation, and this has never been more apparent than in the twentieth century.

While this objection is compelling enough when applied to the past, it is almost irrelevant when applied to the present. It is almost irrelevant to the prospect of war between the superpowers today because such a war would be one of miscalculation in a sense heretofore unknown. Given their speed and destructiveness, nuclear-missile weapons enable men to see the future as they have never before been able to see it. Accordingly, the calculations, and miscalculations, that once extended over years now extend over hours or, at most, days. The uncertainties that formerly attended the decision for war, and that did so as late as World War II, have been replaced by the certainties attending nuclear war between the superpowers. For what remains uncertain about such war is not the minimum extent of destruction each would suffer but whether this destruction will permit the semblance of national life and cohesiveness in its wake. This is not the question national leaders literally asked themselves in 1914, or, for that matter, in 1939. And even if they had done so, they were saved from the direct and brutal answer nuclear weapons present to the statesman.

Seeing the future as they have never before been permitted to see it, statesmen may be expected to resist accepting it more determinedly than they have ever resisted before. Even so, a risk of miscalculation will remain. It will remain so long as the possibility remains that in a severe crisis the moment may come when circumstances conspire to make nuclear war appear inevitable. Logically, that time should never come. If no outcome of a crisis could be worse for either side than the outcome for both represented by nuclear war, neither side should ever be tempted to miscalculate. Given this expectation, it may—indeed, should—be impossible for either side to provoke the other short of an actual strike, in which case there can be no war. This is as close a description of the condition assumed by mutual assured destruction as one need make. But the danger, as we know, is that this logic will break down in a severe crisis, and that one or both sides will become increasingly persuaded of the inevitability of nuclear war. Once that persuasion takes hold a very different logic becomes operative. If nuclear war is considered inevitable, there still may be no advantage gained by striking first (though, again, there may). But the temptation to believe otherwise may prove almost irresistible. If nuclear war is thought to be inevitable, it may prove impossible to resist concluding that there is an advantage in striking first, if only because one might somehow survive the retaliatory blow in a meaningful manner.

However it may arise, it is the conclusion of inevitability that is decisive. That conclusion is of necessity a miscalculation in the sense that if each party had sufficient information about the other party's intentions, there would be no nuclear war. For each would then know that the other had no intention of striking first. Neither party, moreover, has anything to gain that is proportionate to what each stands to lose by obscuring or, what is worse, misrepresenting its intentions. It may be that, short of a severe crisis and the moment of truth to which it is likely to lead, an advantage of sorts can be gained by appearing to have a greater propensity for risk-taking. But to press for such advantage in conditions of a severe crisis would be imprudent in the extreme.

These considerations suggest that the most promising arms control measures are those whose principal purpose is to enable each side in a crisis to have as much access as possible to the intentions and actions of the other side. Short of preventing crises from arising in the first place, it is this form of enhancement of crisis stability that holds out the best prospect of reducing the risk of nuclear war. In turn, it is the mutual reassurance of the participants through what have come to be known as confidence-building measures that is the key to crisis stability. Such reassurance does not and cannot resolve crises. It merely affords the indispensable condition for avoiding one particular outcome of crises.

Measures designed to enhance crisis stability have seldom evoked the interest, let alone the enthusiasm, either of publics or of elites. Instead, it has been the effort to limit the numbers and types of weapons that has done so and, in consequence, that has dominated the arms control process. Yet the result of that effort can scarcely be judged impressive, and this is so even if we grant much of the case made by its supporters. The principal claim made on behalf of the arms control process over the past decade and a half is, indeed, one we have no reliable way of testing. For it consists in the favorable comparison of where we are today with where we might have been in the absence of that process. We cannot know, however, where we might have been without SALT I and II. It may well be that we would not find ourselves in a very different position from the one we find ourselves in today.

Even if this conclusion does less than justice to the record of achievement, it is increasingly apparent that the obstacles to further agreements of the kind earlier reached have now become very considerable. These obstacles are both political and technological and they make the prospects of reaching arms control agreements in the mold of SALT I and II marginal. Moreover, these agreements, even if they could be achieved, would not have the effect of materially reducing the risk of nuclear war. For that risk is not greatly affected by numbers of weapons, and to the extent it is affected by types of weapons, this is as much a function of reaction time as it is of anything else. But reaction time becomes particularly important in periods of crisis. We are thus driven back to the need to devise means whereby the danger of miscalculation in crisis might be progressively reduced to a point that approaches the risk today of accidental nuclear war in peacetime. Once a substantial risk, the chances of accidental nuclear war in non-crisis conditions have now been reduced to close to the vanishing point.[18]

The enhancement of crisis stability would not transform the relationship of mutual deterrence. But the transformation of

18. Paul Bracken notes that "the success of managing the problem of accidental nuclear war in peacetime contrasts with the difficulty of doing so in a crisis. The differences are considerable, for in a crisis our expectation of attack increases, and many of the peacetime controls that prevent accidental war are removed when strategic and theatre forces are placed on alert. That, after all, is what it means to go on alert." "A Way to Avoid an 'Accidental' War," *The Washington Post*, January 6, 1985, p. C8.

mutual deterrence, let alone its abolition, is either beyond our present power of achievement through technological means (SDI) or beyond our desire to achieve through a radical change of policy (withdrawal). The most we may reasonably aspire to in the foreseeable future is a substantial reduction of the risk of nuclear war by measures which do not encounter the obstacles that have beset the arms control process in the recent past. Even if taken, however, these measures might not reduce the fear of nuclear war. At once quite technical in character and modest in appearance, they might not restore the public's faith in deterrence. The ironic prospect, and dilemma, must be faced that what may prove the most promising course for reducing the risk of nuclear war may nevertheless leave unresolved the lapse of faith that provoked the great nuclear debate of this decade.

About the Author

ROBERT W. TUCKER is Professor of International Law and Diplomacy at The Johns Hopkins School of Advanced International Studies and President of The Lehrman Institute. He is the author of numerous books on international politics and U.S. foreign policy, including *Nation or Empire: The Debate over American Foreign Policy; The Radical Left and American Foreign Policy; The Inequality of Nations; The Fall of the First British Empire: Origins of the War of American Independence;* and *The Purposes of American Power.* His essays appear regularly in leading periodicals.